Praise for
Navigating Transitions

Navigating Transitions is an authoritative guide to unlocking the power of purpose by embracing life's most difficult moments. Based on a lifetime of experience, it offers practical value and comfort for anyone facing the trials of transition.

—**Richard Leider**, international bestselling author of *The Power of Purpose*

Navigating Transitions is a compassionate, wise guide for inevitable transitions. We are not designed to go through life-altering changes alone, and Linda Burks is a thoughtful and supportive companion. This book is a testimony to human resilience and is grounded in Linda's lived experiences of transitions. She is a steady hand during turbulent times.

—**Mary NurrieStearns**, psychotherapist, yoga teacher, and author of *Healing Anxiety, Depression and Unworthiness*

Recognizing that life's greatest challenges are at points of transition, Dr. Linda Burks offers not only insightful, instructive narrative and storytelling in *Navigating Transitions*, but practical tools—self-reflective exercises and meditations—that can help us transform those difficult challenges into opportunities for fulfillment.

—**Meredith Woodruff**, founder, COPIA Coaching and Consulting

NAVIGATING TRANSITIONS

NAVIGATING TRANSITIONS

EMBRACING CHANGE AND FINDING PURPOSE

LINDA BURKS, PhD

EMERALD LAKE
BOOKS
Sherman, Connecticut

Navigating Transitions: Embracing Change and Finding Purpose

Copyright © 2025 Linda Burks

Cover © 2025 Emerald Lake Books

All rights reserved. No part of this book may be used or reproduced by any means, graphic, electronic or mechanical, including photocopying, recording, taping or by any information storage retrieval system, without the written permission of the publisher except in the case of brief quotations embodied in critical articles and reviews.

Scriptures taken from the Holy Bible, New International Version®, NIV®. Copyright © 1973, 1978, 1984, 2011 by Biblica, Inc.™ Used by permission of Zondervan. All rights reserved worldwide. zondervan.com. The "NIV" and "New International Version" are trademarks registered in the United States Patent and Trademark Office by Biblica, Inc.™

David Whyte, "Sweet Darkness" from *The House of Belonging*. © 1997 David Whyte. Reprinted with permission from David Whyte and Many Rivers Company, LLC, Langley, WA. davidwhyte.com.

Books published by Emerald Lake Books may be ordered through your favorite booksellers or by visiting emeraldlakebooks.com.

Library of Congress Cataloging-in-Publication Data

Names: Burks, Linda, 1944- author

Title: Navigating transitions : embracing change and finding purpose / Linda Burks, PhD.

Description: Sherman, Connecticut : Emerald Lake Books, [2025] | Includes bibliographical references.

Identifiers: LCCN 2025022861 (print) | LCCN 2025022862 (ebook) | ISBN 9781945847875 trade paperback | ISBN 9781945847882 epub

Subjects: LCSH: Self-actualization (Psychology) | Stress (Psychology)--Prevention | Life change events

Classification: LCC BF637.S4 B874 2025 (print) | LCC BF637.S4 (ebook) | DDC 158.1--dc23/eng/20250805

LC record available at https://lccn.loc.gov/2025022861

LC ebook record available at https://lccn.loc.gov/2025022862

To my reader, I wish you courage on your quest for wholeness.

Table of Contents

Navigating Transitions xv

Chapter 1: Understanding Life's Transformations 1

    Developmental Stages and Challenges 2

    First Half of Life Transitions 3

    Second Half of Life Transitions 4

    Life's Final Transitions 7

    Our Birthright Nature 10

        Soulful Self-Reflection: Claiming Your Birthright Nature 11

Chapter 2: Beginning with Endings 15

    My Transformational Journey 17

    Your Transitional Wounds 18

        Soulful Self-Reflection: Acknowledging Your Wise Heart 23

Chapter 3: Reclaiming Your Authentic Self 25

    Soulful Self-Reflection: Embracing Your True Self 29

    Healthy Boundaries 30

        Setting Clear Boundaries Exercise 33

        Soulful Self-Reflection: Healing Your Relationships 34

Chapter 4: Hearing Your Inner Voice 37
Soulful Self-Reflection: Hearing the Voice Inside the Beat 42
Alexis's Transformational Choice 44
Courageous Conversations Can Heal 48
Soulful Self-Reflection: Starting Courageous Conversations 50

Chapter 5: Trusting the Unfolding 53
Soulful Self-Reflection: Trusting Spirit's Pruning Hand 55

Chapter 6: Bridging Endings to New Beginnings 59
Elizabeth's Revelations from the Soul 62
Your Intuitive Self 65
The Need for Silence 70
Creating a Sacred Refuge 71

Chapter 7: Nurturing Harmony in the Everyday 75
Breath: The Spirit of Life 77
Simple Breath Awareness Practice 79
Soulful Self-Reflection: Following the Journey of the Breath 80

Chapter 8: Practicing Inner Knowing Through Contemplation 83
Just Sitting Meditation 86
Mindfulness Meditation 87
A Contemplative Path to Inner Knowing 89
Soulful Self-Reflection: Practicing the Lectio Divina 90
Poetry as a Sacred Practice 92
Journaling: A Healing and Creative Expression 94
Soulful Self-Reflection: Healing through Journaling 96

Chapter 9: Accepting Change, Trusting the Soul 101
Threads of Continuity 104
Life's Endings and Beginnings 107

Soulful Self-Reflection: Finding Transitional Wisdom 108

Your Soul's Compass 110

Soulful Self-Reflection: Learning from Your Life Journey 110

Chapter 10: Transforming Through Adversity 115

Unexpected Life-Altering Transitions 117

Soulful Self-Reflection: Finding the Purpose in Everything 120

The Heroic Quest for Wholeness 121

The Art of Claiming Your True Self 124

Soulful Self-Reflection: Digging For Treasure in the Ashes 125

Chapter 11: Exploring Passion, Purpose and New Territory 129

Soulful Self-Reflection: Living with Passion and Purpose 134

The Threshold Into New Territory 135

Soulful Self-Reflection: Enjoying the Rapture of Being Alive 137

Jessi's Grit and Grace 138

The Promise of New Beginnings 141

Soulful Self-Reflection: Shining Light in the Inner Wilderness 142

The Honoring of Sacred New Beginnings 144

Chapter 12: Navigating Monumental Transitions 147

Solidarity and Shared Compassion 149

Hope for a Brighter Tomorrow 153

Chapter 13: Moving Forward with Wisdom 157

The Art of Beginnings 158

Discussion Guide 161

Acknowledgments 167

About the Author 169

Navigating Transitions

Life is a complicated tapestry of endings and beginnings. Change is natural and inevitable. We often experience our greatest challenges during major life transitions, when what once was familiar can suddenly seem unfamiliar. We're left feeling apprehensive and uncertain of what lies ahead. While it's natural to want to resist or avoid those uncomfortable feelings, ignoring them doesn't change what's happening.

When we acknowledge life's cyclical nature, we may be surprised to learn that whatever is unfolding is an invitation to explore new and exciting possibilities. As Heraclitus, a pre-Socratic philosopher in fifth-century BC, wrote, "Everything is and is not, for everything is fluid, is constantly changing, constantly coming into being and passing away." To live consciously is to awaken to these changes in our lives and embrace them, not as unwanted and uninvited interruptions, but as unique opportunities to discover who we truly are, what our purpose is in the world, and what is inherently meaningful to us.

To learn how to be masters of our inner landscape, we must accept we have little control over our outer landscape. This transformational process requires a conscious search inward with an inquisitive spirit, while remaining focused on the outward life we are living. Every transition offers the potential for us to gain timeless wisdom. *Navigating Transitions: Embracing Change and Finding Purpose* is about how we respond to adversity, learn to embrace healing and transformational wisdom, and find our passion and purpose.

Change begins within, inside our own hearts and minds. Ancient Greek traditions proposed there are two challenges we face in life: "everything changes" and "know thyself." Whenever transitions occur in our outer world, we experience a corresponding shift in our interior world—in our consciousness. This is usually brought about by some destabilizing event or life transition that shakes us to our core. These occasions might bring us deep pain or intense joy, devastating loss or elated achievement, a sense of overwhelming failure or triumphant success; each of which forces us to reorder, modify, adjust and understand our life in a new way.

When opportunities beckon, you must bravely descend into the depths of your inner being and seek out the lessons these transitions offer. Learning to navigate your inner landscape requires focusing on the stirrings deep within the wilderness of your soul.

Every change is an invitation to pay attention to things as they truly are and assess what really matters in life. Listening honestly to the thoughts and desires whispered by your inner voice does not mean abruptly quitting your job, leaving your relationship, or moving across the country. It means:

- looking at how you live your life or interact in your relationships
- taking yourself seriously
- creating space for other options
- comprehending your life in a new and different way

Even the act of listening with an inquisitive spirit to your inner voice can be a signal that there is more to life than you have known or allowed yourself to imagine.

When you consciously seek to expand and explore your awareness, then deeply held truths, hopes, dreams and desires can reveal themselves. A shift of consciousness requires the integration of your old identity into your new identity, your old reality into your new reality. Transitions provide time to reevaluate your core beliefs, reclaim forgotten dreams, set different goals, explore new desires, and, if necessary, correct course to align with your new life circumstances. As you orient toward your true nature, you discover the gifts of self-knowledge, innate confidence, and a greater sense of purpose and meaning.

Understanding yourself promotes a feeling of wholeness and confidence that whatever is unfolding is an invitation to a new and exciting pathway or an unexpected horizon to explore. Believing your tomorrows can be more fulfilling and meaningful fosters hope and courage today. Over time, transitions mark the milestones in your life story, and you begin to gain the wisdom needed to navigate future changes.

As a licensed psychologist with over four decades of professional clinical experience, I have witnessed firsthand the courage and strength it takes to embrace change and find purpose. I have learned that humans are remarkably resilient and remain capable of transformation throughout their lifetimes. While each journey is unique and personal, there are universal transitions we all encounter.

When I began working on this book, I didn't know what truths I carried in my heart that would be revealed along the way. Writing became an act of hope, courage and discovery, and I trusted that the offerings of love and light hidden beneath the surface would gradually emerge.

Then, in the midst of writing, the world was catapulted into a crisis: the COVID-19 pandemic. Not since the Spanish Flu epidemic in 1918 had the global community experienced such a widespread and catastrophic health emergency. Our lives, as we knew them, seemed to unravel around us. We were forced to face the human condition and confront the roots of our suffering, as both our inner and outer worlds were thrown into a state of chaos and confusion. All of humanity felt the impact of the changes that were needed to keep everyone safe and alive. Our daily existence felt like science fiction. We all longed to return to a time when the news was boring, politics put us to sleep, and no one knew what an epidemiologist was.

But we could not go back to the past, nor could we recover the future we had imagined for ourselves just a few months earlier. We struggled to come to grips with the reality that life would never return to our "old normal." In a state of disbelief and shock, we were forced to dismantle the myth that we were somehow in control of our lives. We were living in extraordinary times and could only speculate about the long-term, fundamental changes required to defeat this invisible enemy. Consequently, writing a book about transitions took on a much broader and urgent purpose for me.

Navigating Transitions offers a wide range of scientific and psychological research, as well as the writing of poets, philosophers, ecumenical scholars, and spiritual teachers from both ancient and modern times, to provide broad cultural and historical perspectives and philosophical depth to the text. The book includes numerous practical self-care principles, evidence-based meditative practices, breathing exercises, guided imagery, and journaling prompts designed to support and encourage self-compassion and self-awareness. These offerings can assist you as you navigate your transitional moments.

I have used my personal stories for illustrative purposes to enrich and enlarge your understanding of how life's struggles can ignite and awaken your consciousness. Three insightful and generous friends have also graciously shared their inspiring experiences. (Names have been changed to honor their privacy.) Sharing personal stories requires more vulnerability than superficial self-disclosure, and I hope these anecdotes illuminate the path for anyone searching for light during a dark night of the soul.

Throughout the book, there are scheduled pauses for Soulful Self-Reflections so you can process the material on your own. These interludes are a time for honest soul-searching and contemplation. Answer the questions and complete the exercises that resonate with you and leave the others for another time or not at all. You may find that some can be completed in a short time with little thought or emotional disturbance, while others evoke intense upset, difficult memories, or require more processing. For that reason, you may wish to wait until you have enough time and energy for the honesty the material deserves. You may also find it helpful to complete the exercises with study partners or a confidential support group to stimulate insightful conversations. The material could also be used in addition to therapy with a trained professional. It is my sincere desire that you use your instincts and judgment and choose the course of action that is the most beneficial and meaningful for you.

One note I want to make is that the word "spirit" has been used simply as a placeholder for what many refer to as the conscious, spiritual presence within all creation. For some, it can signify the Holy Spirit, God, Allah, Yahweh, Jehovah or Brahman. For others, it can represent the teachings of the Buddha-nature or the Indigenous tribal wisdom of the Great Spirit. Or it can honor the collective human spirit or the underlying creative energy that binds all life together. *Navigating Transitions* is an invitation open to all, and every spiritual journey is welcome.

Perhaps you are navigating uncharted waters in the midst of a transitional crisis. Or you may be feeling restless and an inner nudge to move in a different direction. You might be emerging from a deep, dark fog, finally able to make sense of your journey. Whether you are experiencing a stormy crisis or traveling smoothly on your life path, I want you to know you are not alone. We have all been where you are.

As a seasoned traveler on my own transformational journey, I have known the joy of celebration and the pain of change. I have searched for light in the darkness and needed guidance during uncertain times to know my true self and my life's purpose. I have rummaged through the dark cellars of my past to refine new core beliefs and restore inner truths. And I have struggled to discard false assumptions and unrealistic expectations that limited my full acceptance of life's abundant love, peace, forgiveness, compassion and joy.

Life is a gift. Each of us is on a unique journey of self-discovery to learn who we are and why we are here. Life is also not linear. Our vision will continually be modified and revisited as we encounter new things and experience changes. Our search for meaning and purpose is essential and sacred. When we dig deep within our souls to identify our authentic selves and our unique place in the world, we begin to live in harmony with our true natures. Each of us must first find the courage to claim our life story and live authentically from it.

It is my humble wish that this book will illuminate the wisdom that resides deep within you. May you discover a deep awareness of the sacredness of your life and experience the courage and compassion to live fully and wholeheartedly. This is an invitation to come home to your soul, the place of true belonging.

Chapter 1
Understanding Life's Transformations

From the moment we're born, life is constantly changing and evolving. The word *change* may conjure up thoughts of new beginnings. But inner transformation more often happens, not when something new begins, but when something ends. These transitions become our greatest teachers—especially when we begin to see how letting go of the past and welcoming new possibilities are interrelated. In those times, we're compelled to reflect on life's deepest questions:

- What is this event teaching me about who I truly am?
- What are the unique gifts I bring to the world?
- What gives my life passion and meaning?
- Who am I?
- What is my life's purpose?

The complexities of this journey of self-discovery require digging deep to gain a new understanding of yourself and your world. Although something external may have ended, as you hold and integrate that experience subconsciously, you find that limitless and enduring wisdom offers relief to the feeling of finality. Your journey inward begins with taking that first courageous step into the unknown, tapping into the innate knowledge that dwells deep within your soul, and opening the door to the inherent knowing of your true nature. When you befriend transitions and ignite this intelligence, adversity calls into being a wiser, more resilient and compassionate version of your true self, and your passion and purpose emerge.

Inner transformation is difficult because it requires us to be truthful about our life story. No matter how solid and secure our lives may seem, the people and circumstances will not remain the same. When you reach a crossroads, when your world has been turned upside down, you may feel disoriented and confused about who you are and why this is happening. You may wake up one morning with a profound feeling of emptiness, haunted by a vague sense that something important is absent or has been undone. Or you may feel prompted to move in a different direction when you don't feel engaged with your passion and purpose.

We have all witnessed the courage it takes to choose growth over fear as we navigate complex circumstances. And we have marveled at what some of us will do to resist change and how we repeat the same old self-defeating patterns. But avoidance and denial do not lessen the pain of transitions and may only serve to reinforce your negative beliefs and the pretenses you have settled for to feel safe.

When you consciously create space, the parts of yourself you have neglected, ignored or otherwise suppressed will reemerge and find expression. Old interests or activities will lose their appeal as new ones arise to take their place. Your life is brought into alignment with your deepest values and ideals. The invisible is made visible. To live wholeheartedly, you must trust that all transitions carry the possibility of personal growth and wholeness.

Developmental Stages and Challenges

You have experienced changes during your lifetime that have molded you into who you are today. Each one has contributed to your strength, courage and wisdom. Although your experiences are personal and unique to you, there are many universal transitions and challenges almost all of us can relate to. Many developmental stages, such as starting school, graduating, entering the workforce, and retirement, occur naturally as we age. Although time may be required to adjust and adapt, we typically navigate these with relative ease. Other events, such as moving to a new city or state, leaving a career position, or becoming an "empty nester," are less celebratory but are important nonetheless because they give shape and value to our lives. Even a positive event, such as achieving a job promotion, receiving an unexpected inheritance, or winning the lottery, may require a period of adjustment afterward.

Life's more turbulent transitions, such as divorce, the death of a loved one, physical violence, natural disaster, or a physical or mental health crisis, are extremely distressing and disruptive and can significantly affect our physical, emotional and spiritual health. All it takes is a lump in the breast or a suspicious prostate exam, a car accident, or another traumatic brush with death, and in the blink of an eye, life as we knew it has changed forever.

The magnitude of these transitions can be measured by the relative shifts that occur in our circumstances, roles and relationships. The event triggers inner disorganization, confusion and psychological upheaval. As a result, the future may seem unimaginable and insurmountable until a shift in your perspective allows your gifts of self-confidence, self-knowledge and wisdom to shine through. When you've done the hard work of processing the changes in your life, you can then develop a road map for navigating the more earth-shattering changes you are sure to encounter.

First Half of Life Transitions

DEVELOPMENTAL TRANSITIONS BEGIN AT BIRTH—the day of our arrival into a world of possibilities. Once we take our first steps and say our first words, a whole new world of exploration and self-expression begins. We reevaluate our identities and relationships throughout our lifetimes as our circumstances change. The first day of school may create uncertainty and trepidation as we leave the security of home and step into a larger community of people and activities. Passing a driver's test or starting a first after-school job opens up a wider landscape of freedom and independence.

After graduation, we bid the security of childhood goodbye and enter young adulthood—a critical developmental period where we establish independence, gain emotional maturity, and set appropriate boundaries based on our personal goals and beliefs, which may differ from our parents' or other important people in our lives. Negotiating independent relationships while also maintaining the emotional and physical familial support required to be stable can create significant psychological distress for everyone involved. Young adults must formulate a career path, explore diverse interpersonal relationship patterns and lifestyle choices, examine their values and beliefs, and create a personal vision for the future.

Transitioning to the adult world and finding full-time employment ushers in the responsibilities of living independently, becoming a competent and productive employee, and being an accountable member of society and the world. Learning to manage financial obligations, establishing lifestyle beliefs and values, and choosing relationship patterns are major developmental milestones that can be tricky to navigate since the choices we make will affect our future success and happiness.

The decision to remain single or commit to a partner requires another redefinition and reorientation of personal identity. Establishing a committed relationship, along with managing the familial dynamics of both partners, involves ongoing negotiations of lifestyles, values, roles and boundaries to ensure stability and success.

Becoming a parent is also a monumental transition. As parents hold their child for the first time, there are overwhelming feelings of awe and wonder together with startling anxiety about the enormity of the responsibility. Parenting requires another redefinition of roles and duties, negotiating differing parenting styles and beliefs, and developing values and strategies for the new family system. Nothing can compare to the joys and heartaches, triumphs and disappointments parents experience as they witness their child grow and develop into a unique individual.

As those children mature and leave home, empty nesters may wonder, *Who am I without kids to focus my attention on?* and *Who is this person I am married to?* The couple may once again need to define and negotiate their new relationship dynamics and adjust to a different home environment.

Second Half of Life Transitions

SOCIETAL EXPECTATIONS FOR HOW WE LIVE our lives have changed enormously over the past century. In previous generations, life after fifty was regarded as a time for retirement and then death. Adulthood was about working hard to achieve success and becoming secure enough to have the time and resources to explore who we truly are, do what we love, and enjoy life. We were programmed to prepare for life rather than enjoy it.

Advances in biomedicine, technology and medical treatment have created a profound change, not only by extending life but also by altering how individuals and society define and adapt to the gift of longevity. While we are living longer, we also have a relatively higher level of good health and energy, more free time and resources, and new ways to engage in society. Adding decades to our life expectancies has forced us to imagine a new framework for the second half of our lives that is very different from the stereotypical roles and expectations of past generations. This unanticipated longevity requires a new cultural perspective, wherein we must explore who we are, what we want and need, and what we have to contribute to society.

In her book *The Third Chapter*, Sara Lawrence-Lightfoot writes:

> We must develop a compelling vision of later life, one that does not assume a trajectory of decline after fifty but recognizes this as a time of potential change, growth and new learning, a time when our courage gives us hope.[1]

Today, we have time to reflect on past transitions and to recognize that it is not too late to do something more or different. This shift in consciousness and identity invites us to broaden our vision for our lives. We have been given the gift of time for new adventures and creative endeavors as we alter our plans for the future and discover exciting aspects of ourselves. Our longevity invites us to embrace the idea that "It's never too late to…"

Life after fifty grants us the chance to reawaken the essence of who we truly are and ignite our creative potential, bringing excitement and meaning to this stage of life. It can be a time for learning new skills and dusting off talents or passions put on the back burner while building a career or raising a family.

Civic engagement and encore careers can also factor into this stage of life. Freud famously said that what gives meaning to life is *lieben und arbeiten*—to love and to work. Rather than sitting idly by on the sidelines or spending time playing golf or bridge, older adults may choose to continue their careers in a slightly reduced capacity or with a flexible work schedule. Alternatively, they may share their expertise by becoming mentors, consultants or teachers, which

---

1 Sara Lawrence-Lightfoot, *The Third Chapter: Passion, Risk, and Adventure in the 25 Years After 50* (Sarah Crichton Books, 2009), 8-9.

enables them to nurture younger people, but also to embrace novelty and stay engaged by learning new things.

People in the second half of life may feel as though they are onstage without a script, tasked with improvising until they learn a different dance. The challenge is developing a more liberated consciousness regarding ageism and retirement that frees the imagination for a new vision for the future. Older adults have a lifetime of experience and expertise with which to create opportunities to remain engaged and contribute to society. Socially valued work, creativity and passion, and a strong desire to give back to the world what they have been given are expressions of what developmental psychologist Erik Erikson described as "generativity vs. stagnation."[2] While generativity refers to a need to nurture and guide younger people, stagnation reflects the slowing down we feel as we age. Reconciling the tension between the two is crucial to our well-being.

Generativity includes using one's energies to teach, advocate, mentor and express creativity. Erikson broadened generativity to include giving something back and paying it forward—leaving a legacy for the betterment of society. Those living the second half of life use their abundance for the benefit of future generations. Richard Rohr, in his book *Falling Upward*, puts it this way: these people "live simply so that others can simply live." By uniting fruitful activity with a deep passion to give back to future generations and society, life becomes not so much "to have what we love," but "to love what we have."[3]

In her book *Composing a Further Life*, Mary Catherine Bateson describes this stage of the life cycle as Adulthood II—a time for improvisation, calling on our imaginations and creativity, and the discovery of unexpected possibilities.[4] This name suggests a period of liberation and freedom. With more time to create, fewer familial and social obligations, and a lessening of inhibitions and fears, Adulthood II offers us permission to do the things that bring joy and meaning to our lives, such as creating our own wild adventures and living life with

---

[2] Erik H. Erikson, Joan M. Erikson, and Helen Q. Kivnick, *Vital Involvement in Old Age: The Experience of Old Age in Our Time* (W. W. Norton & Company, 1986), 73.

[3] Richard Rohr, *Falling Upward: A Spirituality for the Two Halves of Life* (Jossey-Bass, 2022), 77–79.

[4] Mary Catherine Bateson, *Composing a Further Life: The Age of Active Wisdom* (Vintage Books, 2010), 19–23.

passion and meaning. When we recognize that life is short, we may experience a heightened sense of urgency—thinking, if not now, then when?

Many of those who are middle-aged and older also have the time, energy and resources to build the kinds of relationships with their grandchildren or great-grandchildren that they may have missed with their own kids due to work responsibilities and caring for hearth and home. Intergenerational exchanges give younger people an opportunity to witness the generativity, adaptations and acquired wisdom of older adults, thus providing them with a road map for the journey ahead. Sharing these lessons with mutual respect and empathy in cross-generational encounters, conversations and projects is vitally important for future generations and society.

Second-half people have seen a lot of change and learned how to adapt through good times and bad. Transitional wisdom refers to the lessons we learn from life experiences and incorporate into our future decisions. Our willingness to affirm the usefulness and value of this wisdom is a gift we can give to the world.

Life's Final Transitions

THE QUEST FOR MEANING ENCOMPASSES most cultures and theologies and often surfaces during life transitions. A passionate soul never dies. We have known people in their nineties who have just as much zest for living as they did in their twenties, simply because they have a deep awareness of their purpose. Having a clear sense of what gives life meaning can have a powerful effect on our physical, mental and spiritual health. It becomes the motivation behind our will to live when faced with overwhelming challenges. Purpose can transform our perspective and help sustain us as we move toward a brighter tomorrow.

When we still feel useful, it connects us with our sense of vitality and is essential to healthy aging. Award-winning author Dan Buettner traveled the world to learn the powerful yet simple lessons to living a longer life. In his book *The Blue Zones*, Buettner visited the five regions in the world with the highest proportions of people who reach the age of 100: Sardinia, Italy; Okinawa, Japan; Ikaria, Greece; Loma Linda, California; and Nicoya, Costa Rica, and interviewed the centenarians who lived there.⁵ The seven-year Blue Zones project found that having a sense of purpose may act as a buffer against stress and reduce inflammation, thus lowering the risk of developing certain health conditions, such as arthritis, stroke and Alzheimer's. In the Blue Zone regions, having purpose was also found to play a major role in one's sense of well-being, adding up to about seven additional years of longevity.⁶ Okinawans call it *ikigai*, a "reason for being," and Costa Ricans call it *plan de vida*, "why I wake up in the morning."

This does not mean we have to save the world or even think in such lofty terms. Blue Zone centenarians reported simple daily activities, such as setting the family dinner table, rocking a great-grandchild, gathering vegetables from the garden, or visiting a friend in need of companionship, as activities that made life meaningful. They put personal connections and family first. Social networks that reinforce good habits, healthy lifestyles, and challenge one's mental abilities can favorably improve health and longevity.⁷ A 107-year-old Sardinian woman, when asked if she had any advice for younger people, responded with, "Yes. Life is short. Don't run so fast you miss it."

Wise elders endeavor to balance the wisdom of what really matters in life with integrity and enduring human wholeness. Our most authentic and powerful legacies come from living with purpose and benefiting others with our unique gifts, guided by a passionate soul. These simple acts—both tangible and intangible—of contributing and being of service are things we need to remain passionate about living.

It is impossible to fully embrace life without accepting the inevitability of change. As an older adult, your experiences and relationships can shift significantly, and unfamiliar responsibilities and roles may emerge that demand adjustments and adaptations. These challenges may require delicate negotiations to reach a "new normal," and honest, respectful, clear communication is critical. By being sensitive to changing physical and emotional needs, we reduce stress and create a caring and loving environment.

As we brave the journey through older adulthood, we may experience a phenomenon known as grieving "ambiguous losses"—a prolonged process that

---

5 Dan Buettner, *Blue Zones: Lessons for Living Longer from the People Who've Lived the Longest* (National Geographic Society, 2008), xxiii.
6 Buettner, *Blue Zones*, 245.
7 Buettner, *Blue Zones*, 249.

is one of the most difficult challenges of life's final phase. We mourn the many lives and relationships we have lost. Some we welcomed and later left behind. Others were taken or ended too soon. Many continue to feed our soul.

Likewise, we might wonder how we have impacted the lives of others. These people may no longer be a part of our life, but their traces remain a part of us forever. It is important to reflect on and give thanks for all the lives and relationships that have enriched and colored our world.

One of the fascinating things about older adulthood is our repository of everything that has ever happened in our lifetime. Nothing is ever lost or forgotten. Similar to the rings of a tree, which mark the cyclical unfolding of the seasons, we can view our memories as markers for the events and experiences of our life. Everything that befalls us is stored in this metaphorical vault. When we have traversed a difficult phase of life or suffered a painful transition, the lessons that emerge can be very enlightening. Diving into our memories allows us to harvest the wisdom that resides deep within our soul.[8]

As a result, these twilight years involve a complex process of retrospection and reconciliation, where we seek to consolidate our wisdom and perspectives while incorporating a lifetime of experiences and events, choices and consequences. By acknowledging and integrating past transitions, present reality, and future uncertainty, this process consciously merges the wisdom gained from maturing forms of purpose, competence, fidelity, hope and love. With this, the life cycle "weaves back on itself in its entirety," integrating a "comprehensive sense of wisdom"[9] as each transitional experience is woven into the fabric of the whole.

As we slow down and reduce our activities, we have more time for contemplating the events and experiences that took place over our lifetimes, and our inner life grows richer and more expansive. We welcome silence and solitude with curiosity and wonder. And with more time and freedom for self-reflection, we discover a new fascination and companionship with our own soul.

In contrast to calendar time, there is eternal time, where the spirit unfolds and deepens. Eternal time becomes possible when we imagine a realm beyond endings, where spirit is alive and complete, where our soul can be released into a

---

8 John O'Donohue, *Walking In Wonder: Eternal Wisdom for a Modern World* (Convergent Books, 2015), 151.
9 Erikson, *Vital Involvement*, 55–56.

realm where there is no more darkness and no more pain. As we gain a sense of inner wholeness, we may also be surprised by joy and peace.[10] When we allow our sacred wisdom to awaken, we gain the courage and calm compassion to strengthen us as we approach death.

The summons of the soul to a more meaningful and purposeful life is what makes us profoundly human and sustains our conscious engagement during life's final transition. Rather than viewing death with dread, it can be a time to claim our spiritual identity and celebrate our life. Imagine what it would be like if we could view our ending not as an unwelcome guest, but as an unseen companion who has been walking with us every step of the way? How would that free us to live with a deeper sense of passion and purpose?

Our Birthright Nature

THE KERNEL OF WHO WE ARE is knit into our innermost being at our making. Just like an acorn knows what it is and grows into an oak tree, our seed contains the beginnings of our spiritual identity, or what we call our "soul."

Your DNA molecules, found inside the nucleus of almost every cell, direct what makes you physically unique—from your hair color to your fingerprints. This customized programming reveals your birthright nature and contains all the instructions your body needs to develop, reproduce and survive. Similarly, your seed of selfhood contains the spiritual DNA for your uniqueness—your undivided, whole, authentic self. It is made up of all the complex qualities and characteristics that are distinct to you. No one else on the planet shares them.

Your birthright nature reveals your unique spiritual identity: who you are, your strengths, gifts, passions and purpose. This wisdom is revealed when you are willing to go in search of your authentic self and purpose. Cultivating and honoring your uniqueness helps fuel the fire for claiming your authentic self, personal gifts, and purpose.

Parker Palmer, a highly respected author, lecturer and activist, writes:
> We are born with a seed of selfhood that contains the spiritual DNA of our uniqueness—an encoded birthright knowledge of who we are, why

---

10 O'Donohue, *Walking In Wonder*, 147–149.

we are here, and how we are related to others.[11]

Thomas Merton called it the true self. Buddhists call it our original nature. Quakers call it the inner teacher or the inner light. Humanists call it identity and integrity. In this book, I refer to it in multiple ways—as our true self, our authentic self, our spiritual identity, or our soul.

There is nothing more beautiful than affirming and validating our unique spiritual DNA. When we have silence and solitude to contemplate our spiritual identity, we are able to trust and honor the eternal wisdom of our undivided, whole, authentic self.

When we embrace our birthright nature, we are gifted with the ability to imagine all the possibilities for celebrating who we truly are and why we were created, which grants us the courage and confidence to endure life's transformational journey to wholeness.

Soulful Self-Reflection: Claiming Your Birthright Nature

Throughout your life, your authentic self is informed by the significant people you encounter and the events you experience. You are influenced by others' expectations, which may have little to do with your spiritual identity. Although their intent may be noble, they affect your selfhood by trying to mold you to fit prescribed cultural and societal roles of acceptability in families, schools, communities and religious organizations. As the years progress, you might abandon your true self, but it remains buried within your soul. For example, when we become a parent, it's easy to get caught up in the demands of that role and the expectations of others to the extent that we lose sight of who we are apart from that role. If you are mindful, you can reclaim it and reveal your unique gifts.

Childhood is when your selfhood is the most intact and closely connected with your spiritual identity. Reflecting on your early memories is one of the best methods for decoding your spiritual DNA: who you are, why you are here, and what your unique gifts are.

Let me share an exercise with you that will allow you to reconnect with the birthright nature you carry deep within you.

---

11 Parker J. Palmer, *A Hidden Wholeness: The Journey Toward An Undivided Life* (Jossey-Bass, 2004), 32–34.

Find a quiet place and settle yourself. Begin by sitting and breathing gently. Inhale long and deep, and then exhale in a slow and relaxed manner. Repeat that a few times. As you breathe in, let the sound and rhythm of your breathing harmonize with your heartbeat. Allow these sensations to lead you into the silence within—your path to wisdom.

Think back over your childhood and pick a specific time when you felt the most alive, free to be your own person, and comfortable in your own skin. Allow yourself to remember those intense emotions, vivid images, delicate details, resounding uncertainties, and the wonderment of that experience. Try to answer these questions:

- Where were you?
- Who was with you?
- Were you alone?

Remember the sounds, smells, sights and emotions associated with that specific childhood memory.

Now, write about a specific recollection that resonates strongly with you. Let your thoughts, feelings and insights flow without explanation or concern about proper grammar or spelling. Listen to your inner voice.

Let your words flow as you recall details of the experience:

- What was going on outwardly?
- What was going on inwardly?
- What were your fears, joys, hopes, dreams at the time?

Write freely about whatever feelings, insights or thoughts arise without judgment, explanation or editing. Trust your memory and stop when you feel it is complete.

After you have finished, use the questions below to gain more insight into your answers:

- What made you think of this particular experience?
- Did you have a difficult time recalling a memory, or did one immediately come to mind?

- What was significant about it?
- Sometimes, when remembering a specific childhood memory, we recall an additional layer we had forgotten, dismissed or denied. Did you? If so, what new images, details and wonderments did you discover or recall today?
- Did this exercise reveal new aspects of your birthright nature to you? If so, what were they?
- How might you reconnect with or claim those unique gifts, qualities and characteristics that are the core of who you are?

Chapter 2
Beginning with Endings

Everything that comes into being changes continually. As seasons flow from one into the other, the beauty and purpose of life's cyclical nature emerges: the promise of spring brings the ripening of summer, and the bounty of autumn's harvest gives way to the mysterious containment of winter. There is no season without worth and beauty. In each one of them, the natural world teaches us the wisdom of change.

The road to wholeness is paved with transformation, which includes relinquishing the past, separating from the familiar, and moving forward into a new beginning. Change is the raw material out of which life is forged. Every transition begins with an ending, often disguised as a painful beginning. The loss of a marriage, the death of a loved one, or simply traversing a developmental milestone ushers in new opportunities for growth and unique experiences. We are continually passing from one chapter to another, losing and gaining people, places, things and ways of being in the world. It is through letting go and moving on that we become fully developed human beings.

All transitions involve some type of ending, which can be far more encompassing and problematic than we initially recognize. We typically associate loss with the death of a loved one. In her book *Necessary Losses*, Judith Viorst expands our understanding of this, saying, "We lose not only through death, but also by leaving and being left, by changing and letting go and moving on." These necessary losses include "our separations and departures from those we love," as well as "conscious and unconscious losses of romantic dreams, impossible expectations, illusions of freedom and power, illusions of safety, and loss of our younger self, the self we thought would always be unwrinkled and invulnerable and immortal."[12]

So what are you to do when life throws a large boulder in your path and you are faced with the weighty choices of how to navigate the transition? There will be countless times when the world seems to stop on its axis and we feel a loss of control. The illusion that we are somehow running the show perpetuates our tendency to deny, avoid or repress our feelings about painful endings. But we suffer greatly when we refuse to acknowledge that change is inevitable. Resistance can lead to stagnation, frustration and fear. Our reluctance to face change—in ourselves, in relationships, in the world—becomes a veil of denial that prevents us from moving forward and experiencing new adventures.

Weighty choices are the significant and messy ones, often disrupting your life and the lives of others. Transitions compel you to ask provocative questions:

- Will you just roll over and go back to sleep?
- Will you put on a false front and pretend everything is just fine?
- Will you keep repeating the same old patterns of relating to other people over and over again?
- Or will you gather your courage, choose to listen to your inner voice, and forge a new path toward personal growth?

During these transformative moments, you must search inward and ask yourself, "Who am I now at this phase in my life? How can I chart a new vision for my future?"

Life's challenges offer a unique opportunity for reevaluating and making choices and often brings both apprehension and excitement as you enter the next chapter. Transitions encourage you to grow beyond your personal limits and make space for exploring new goals, cultivating different choices, creating alternative interests, or reclaiming forgotten dreams. You must affirm the changes and embrace how each has contributed to who you are today.

---

12 Judith Viorst, *Necessary Losses: The Loves, Illusions, Dependencies, and Impossible Expectations That All of Us Have to Give Up in Order to Grow* (Simon and Schuster, 1986), 15.

Endings bring you to the edge of new beginnings, which are fertile ground for new possibilities, grand adventures, and exciting opportunities waiting just over the horizon. They are the threshold to a new world—a new vision you could never have imagined without prompting. As the Tao Te Ching advises us, "If you realize that all things change, there is nothing you will try to hold on to."[13] Recognizing this truth, we can hold in our heart appreciation and gratitude for both the past and future. When you have hope and a vision to work toward, you can courageously move beyond the present and begin your quest to embrace change and find purpose.

My Transformational Journey

AN UNINVITED LIFE EVENT SPARKED my transformational journey, which led me to my professional vocation and a lifelong quest for self-discovery. Confronted with a life-altering change, I began my search for "Who am I?" and "What is my purpose?" Let me share a bit of the backstory of my first major transition.

I grew up in a small Midwestern rural community, the second daughter in an intact, stable, loving, middle-class family. My father, a traveling salesman, was away from home Monday through Friday throughout my life, while my mother, a shy, anxious, stay-at-home mom, was devoted to her two daughters and her aging parents in her role as caretaker. Family, church and school were the primary focus of my childhood.

I never remember having a serious conversation about going to college or being asked about my aspirations for the future. Growing up in the 1950s, with its gender norms, and watching Disney's Cinderella and Snow White being rescued by their Prince Charmings, my assumption was that I would marry my high school sweetheart, work to put him through college, have two children, and—as promised by all the fairy tales—live happily ever after.

After a seven-year marriage, my idealized life unraveled when it ended in divorce. I became clinically depressed and was devastated by this life-altering crisis. My family physician referred me to a licensed psychologist, Dr. Julia McHale, who quite literally changed my life trajectory forever.

---

13 Lao Tzu, *Tao Te Ching: An Illustrated Journey*, trans. Stephen Mitchell (Frances Lincoln Limited, 1999), 74.

As I walked out of Dr. McHale's office after my first therapy session, I realized that somehow, in the space of an hour, I had gone from being scared to death about what was happening and wondering how I was going to survive to feeling more hopeful about the future and confident about making a new life for myself and my two young children.

Dr. McHale was the first person ever to ask me, "What do you want for your life?" For the first time, I had experienced the transformative power of the right words at the right moment. They awakened my confidence and courage. Although nothing had changed in my outer world, my inner world seemed brighter, and I felt emotionally and spiritually lighter. A shift of consciousness occurred, and my transformational journey began.

At that time, my two children were the force behind my motivation to do whatever was necessary to make a new life. I was determined to ensure they had a secure, loving home where they could grow to their full potential. Armed with this attitude, I was ready to transform adversity into opportunity.

With only a few university credit hours and working part-time with very limited financial resources, I secured student loans and began my academic and professional journey to become a licensed clinical psychologist. I wanted to help others who were going through turbulent transitions, just as Dr. McHale had guided me through my major life crisis over several sessions. Her words of encouragement and enlightenment started me down a path of lifelong self-discovery, in pursuit of knowing who I am and living my life with purpose.

My transition taught me that when we can find meaning in life's vicissitudes, our consciousness expands and we emerge from the darkness into the light. My transformation led me to a meaningful vocation that has brought me purpose throughout my life. I learned lessons from the trials and tribulations I faced that have become my guiding light through dark times.

Your Transitional Wounds

WE WILL EXPERIENCE MANY TURBULENT transitions throughout our lifetime: the loss of a failed relationship, a life-altering diagnosis, betrayal and broken trust, and even deep grief resulting from death. We have all suffered through the pain of change. Life is never exactly as we planned or hoped it would be. Who are we to assume we are exempt from its turbulent transitions? We all have those moments when we ask: "Why is this happening? What am I meant to do with my pain and grief, my fear and disillusionment, my anger and resentment?"

Smooth and calm rarely describe the overwhelming emotions we experience when a major disruption occurs. Some changes happen unexpectedly, with no preparation. We are often left disturbed and bereft when something happens and, in an instant, life as we know it is turned upside down. In that moment, we may feel lost, in shock, or overwhelmed with emotions, wondering how we will survive. We may cry out, "That's not fair!" which only serves to keep us stuck in our pain, fear, frustration and anger; our reaction is a waste of our precious time and energy.

Other times, we feel ambushed, even though there may have been warning signs and signals. We simply chose to deny or ignore the inevitability of the ending in order to believe we are secure in our well-ordered life. Saying "I don't want things to be this way" is a futile attempt to control what is happening and resist the pain.

Some transitions move slowly. It may take a considerable amount of time before we grasp the reality that everything has become stagnant and the drudgery of just getting through the day leaves us feeling weary and hopelessly stuck.

Regardless of how we view them, transitions have a way of violently shaking the ground beneath our feet. We may worry, complain and resist life's ever-changing landscape, only to discover that if we avoid, ignore or deny the reality of what is happening during these dark nights of the soul, we make our grief, loss and spiritual crisis worse. These responses may temporarily diminish the loneliness and anguish by forcing the pain of change out of our mind, but when the thoughts and feelings return, as they always do, the emotions will only become stronger and consume more of our energy and time.

Human beings will often do anything to avoid physical and emotional discomfort. We may try to stay busy in an effort not to experience the pain of change. Alternatively, we may panic when there is nothing or nobody to distract us. We may even pretend everything is "just fine" to avoid the reality that life is changing, despite our efforts to control what is happening. However, distress may be the only way to gain our full attention and disrupt any thinking patterns that might delude us into believing we can miraculously control reality.

Although you are not responsible for all the changes that may befall you, you are responsible for how you respond. You must claim your unique pain and the truth your woundedness reveals. Seek to understand what your struggles are teaching you about who you truly are and what gives life meaning and purpose. The question you need to ask yourself is: "How do I embrace change and find my purpose?" It is only when you honestly own your pain and take responsibility for understanding it that you experience true freedom.

In a culture that prescribes a quick fix for any discomfort, we are not likely to find the idea of enlightenment through suffering very appealing. With all the emphasis on feeling good, we would just as soon avoid anything coming from the darker side of the emotional menu. If you grew up in an environment where feelings were ignored, denied or met with disdain or punishment, you may also develop the unconscious belief that only "good" emotions are permissible. Your more distressing ones may have been labeled unacceptable, and perhaps you were even taught they were not permitted. Over time, you learned to categorize your feelings as good or bad, right or wrong, when truthfully, it is not the emotions that are negative, but other people's attitudes toward them.

Being alive means you will experience complex and mixed emotions, all of which—both light and dark—exist together. Joy and sorrow, love and anger, excitement and fear, laughter and tears are natural and normal responses to the situations and relationships we encounter every day. We grieve because what connects us to other people also breaks our hearts.

But when you consciously lean into these so-called negative emotions and let them wash over and through you, you'll begin to recognize their benefits. Out of sorrow, the unexpected gift of gratitude for life itself eventually breaks forth. Fear alerts you to threats and danger. And when you befriend fear and accept your vulnerability, you expand your capacity for courage and compassion. Despair asks you to cut through the illusions, repair your wounded soul, and find meaning that will sustain you through difficult times.

Our dark emotions may be unwelcome guests when they arrive, but they are just as human as love, joy and wonder. When you accept that your sorrows as much a part of life as your joys, you realize emotions are not your adversaries. In fact, every one of them exists in every moment of your life. Your negative emotions only worsen in intensity and duration when you avoid or repress what is happening and deny how you are honestly feeling.

When you do not honor your darker emotions, you may end up experiencing their displaced and destructive forms, such as depression, anxiety, phobias and self-destructive behaviors. Rather than engaging in unhealthy, energy-robbing attempts to avoid and deny what you're feeling, you must try to understand their source. These negative emotions are a part of who you are, just as surely as the positive ones. That's simply part of being human. But when you accept the full spectrum of your emotions without judgment, you are accepting your true nature.

Discernment is an essential skill for befriending the darker side of your life. The root word "discern" comes from the Latin *discernere*, meaning to separate or divide. While you may have hidden your emotions and irrational beliefs, hoping they would go away, unfortunately, they will not. You must learn to use discernment to sift out what is relevant and glean insight from your experiences.

The process depends on cultivating three basic skills:

1. consciously attending to and naming your darker emotions, irrational beliefs, and unhealthy patterns of relating that keep you stuck in the past;
2. discarding and reprogramming old roles, interests and activities while sowing new dreams, goals and relationships;
3. consciously claiming the fullness of your true nature.

Once you discover the source of these emotions and beliefs, and learn to recognize and trust in your worth and inner truth, your restless spirit can find rest.[14]

Dare to embrace your darker emotions. By acknowledging pain and courageously living through it, you will discover that it will not destroy you. Human brokenness is not a fatal condition. When you stop resisting and face your wounds, you emerge with more strength, humility and courage than ever imagined.[15] Over time, you slowly gain a confidence that serves to strengthen your reserve. Old fears will seem to fade, and you'll discard beliefs you've

---

14 Henri Nouwen, *Discernment: Reading the Signs of Daily Life* (HarperCollins Publishers, 2013), 183.

15 Nouwen, *Discernment*, 135–137.

outgrown. Discernment allows you to relinquish your old patterns of relating and abandon lifestyle choices that no longer satisfy you or bring pleasure.

The key to understanding whether your darker feelings are destructive or transformative is whether you can peer fearlessly into the shadows. To live fully, you must claim the totality of your experiences. If you can befriend your darkness, treating it like a familiar guest rather than a threatening stranger, your life will become significantly different. When you own your struggles, you will feel solidarity with the rest of humanity's striving and will be able to offer courage, hope and compassion, not only to yourself, but to others.

As you accept that emotions are natural responses to the situations you encounter in life, you will begin to reclaim your ability to feel. Restoring your emotional balance begins with paying attention to the subtle currents and impulses that flow through your body, mind and spirit. When you descend to the bottom of your grief and loss, into the darkness of your pain, you gain the confidence to overcome your fears and risk reaching out in love and accepting it in return. In other words, when you lower your protective barrier, you consciously connect with your inner knowing and become more in tune with other people and the world. Becoming gentler toward yourself allows you to become gentler and more accepting of others. Compassion and love form the foundation of all healthy, caring relationships and are critical for achieving inner and outer balance and wholeness.

But in moments of intense suffering, you may lose touch with the ability to offer yourself that grace. By first practicing self-compassion, you will find not only a way to hold your struggles and sorrows in your heart, but connect with the suffering and sorrows of those around you.

When you feel sad and lonely, when you long to be comforted, it is time to enter spirit's compassionate heart, where all suffering is embraced in unconditional love and compassion. When you journey inward, it allows you to experience empathy for yourself and all humanity. You return to the divine light, where "everything exposed by the light becomes visible—and everything that is illuminated becomes a light." (Ephesians 5:13). You simply have to be still and wait for spirit to shine light and love on your inner knowing.

If this practice seems unfamiliar to you, in this exercise, I will provide some guidance for becoming more self-accepting.

Soulful Self-Reflection: Acknowledging Your Wise Heart

If you're experiencing a difficult change, you may ask yourself: "How do I remain sane when everything around me seems to be falling apart? How do I survive in the midst of an unbearable loss? What am I supposed to learn from this?"

Present within our spiritual DNA lies our "wise heart," which is the wisdom of our authentic self. Regardless of what is happening externally, this core awareness remains.

When you courageously search within, your wise heart can provide a gentle welcome and calm assurance for your wounded spirit. It knows your anger, sadness and fear are all part of a normal grieving process.

Surviving a painful transition reassures you that you can face future adversity. Change and loss will still bring overwhelming pain and grief, but you'll discover you can move forward with greater insight and wisdom, more courage and strength, and deeper faith when you connect with your wise heart.

Let me share a meditation with you that is designed to invite your wise heart to share the wisdom you acquired during a difficult time in your life.

> Find a quiet place and settle yourself. Begin by sitting and breathing gently, inhaling long and deep and then exhaling in a slow and relaxed manner. Allow yourself to be led to the silence within.
>
> Now, remember a time in your life when you experienced a painful transition or something changed or ended. Notice your feelings as you recall this difficult event. If they become overwhelming, bring your awareness back to your breathing. Gently pat your heart and belly to calm and comfort yourself.
>
> Allow your wise heart, your wisdom, to offer you courage and strength as you recall how you survived this challenging time. Acknowledge the insights you gleaned from this tumultuous experience.
>
> If you are currently in the midst of a difficult life transition, invite your wise heart to join you as you move forward through the situation. Bask in its calming presence and recognize your deep connection with it as you progress through your journey.

As you meditate, ask yourself these questions:

- What thoughts surfaced for you?
- What feelings did it bring up?
- What insights did you gain from reflecting on this experience?

Write freely about whatever feelings, insights or thoughts arise without judgment, explanation or editing. Trust your memory and stop when you feel it is complete.

Now, describe how this information will be helpful either in your current stressful situation or during future turbulent transitions. Identify ways you can strengthen your connection with your wise heart to receive the infinite wisdom available to you throughout your lifetime.

Every transition is a unique opportunity for self-discovery and transformational wisdom. You may never silence all your fears, but you can make your journey one that is more courageous and compassionate by following your wise heart.

Chapter 3
Reclaiming Your Authentic Self

Your most sacred relationship is the one you have with yourself. At the same time, you are often a stranger to who you truly are. You may ask yourself, "What do I think, how do I feel, or why do I act in such a way?"—only to have no substantial response. You know little or nothing about your deepest thoughts, emotions, intuitions and desires, making you a stranger in your own home. Becoming whole begins with trusting your inner truth and claiming your authentic self.

Developing a healthy sense of being happens through self-discovery and awareness of your personal autonomy within your relationships, social and cultural norms, and societal history and context. This process requires having a safe place where your authentic self is honored and valued and where you are free to communicate your inner truth.

The experience of being loved and cared for nurtures the expression of your authentic self, which manifests in a sense of self-worth, security and stability. The goal is to feel calm, centered and focused on your thoughts, emotions, needs and desires. When you are secure, it enables you to have healthy interactions with others.

Love and relationships are the guiding forces in our lives. As children, we relate to the world by imitating those around us. Our first models are our parents, extended family members, teachers and the culture we grow up in. We identify with and shape our behaviors to imitate them, hoping to receive love and acceptance. These influences can affect our personality, our ability to trust ourselves and others, our sense of self-worth and self-respect, and our personal autonomy well into adulthood.

Self-awareness and autonomy begin in early childhood when language emerges. By using your words, "yes" or "no," "I want to" or "I don't want to," you give voice to your needs, desires, feelings and thoughts, thereby reinforcing your independence and allowing you to feel a greater sense of control over your world. Having this freedom allows you to develop a sense of who you are and what makes you unique. If your independence is thwarted during this crucial stage of development, you can become stuck—either by holding on too tightly or submitting too easily to others. To avoid pain and discomfort, fear of rejection, disapproval or abandonment may lead to a pattern of pleasing others or being a "good girl/boy."

Love is the most intense of human emotions and also the most vulnerable. Basic human fears involve rejection and loss of love. Your self-worth, behaviors and feelings are conditioned by the presence or absence of love and approval from significant people in your life. For example, you may have received validation from one parent when you were growing up, but were ridiculed by the other. As a result, you received the subtle message that something was wrong with you. Consequently, you may have adopted the belief that you were not smart enough, pretty enough, or athletic enough to be successful. As children, we trust others' judgment and insight, and these subtle negative messages of not being acceptable directly affect our sense of self-worth. When you do not receive ample love and acceptance and your basic needs for security are unmet, your authentic self is buried beneath fear, uncertainty and confusion. Consequently, the early childhood developmental process of separation-individuation, where the child develops a distinct and independent sense of self, separate from their primary caregiver, is never fully accomplished.

If you grew up in a home where pleasing others or being the "good kid" was your only way to gain attention or love, you may fail to learn the difference between real love and people-pleasing. If you're living in fear of emotional rejection, disapproval and abandonment, you may unconsciously ignore your natural instincts and never learn how to respond to and honor your emotional needs. As a result, you may try to find a sense of security by telling yourself that things are good enough, rather than taking responsibility for fulfilling your passions and dreams.

An excessive need to please others may manifest in the development of unconscious, internalized beliefs, like *I am not worthy of love and attention.* Unrealistic expectations to be perfect and please others can lead to a lifetime of chronic caretaking, overachievement and perfectionism, which results in exhaustion, depression and interpersonal relationship problems. And if carried into adulthood, these internalized beliefs negatively impact having a secure sense of self and a genuine sense of self-worth.

Codependence is defined as a loss of selfhood. It is a condition where your sense of being loved, accepted and worthy may be based solely on pleasing others and being perfect. When you relinquish your authentic self to others through codependent caretaking and appeasing behaviors, you also relinquish your self-respect, emotional security, independence and integrity. Gaining the approval of others becomes more important than satisfying your own needs. When you allow others to define you, you lose touch with your personal beliefs, thoughts, feelings, decisions, choices and even your physical sensations. When you disown your authentic self, you are unable to realize your potential and recognize your worth and uniqueness.

Events in early childhood shape and affect the way we make sense of our experiences later in life. Your brain's internal operating system interprets your current circumstances through the lens of your early years. This includes your explanation of the events of your life and, most importantly, turbulent situations, such as adoption, the death of a significant person, parental divorce, physical and emotional illness, domestic violence, sexual abuse, or gun violence. These experiences can trigger significant disorientation and disequilibrium related to survival and security.[16]

As a result, you develop coping strategies for how to deal with the world, how it works, and your place in it. These become hard-wired as unconscious, internalized beliefs, such as *I am unlovable, People are untrustworthy,* or *Don't get close to anyone because they will eventually leave you.* Your subsequent

---

16 Bessel van der Kolk, *The Body Keeps the Score: Brain, Mind, and Body In the Healing of Trauma* (Penguin Books, 2014), 349–353.

experiences may be interpreted through the lens of this distorted belief system, and you are likely to respond to future transitions with the same outdated, self-sabotaging behavior patterns that keep you stuck in past woundedness.

If you identify strongly with these unconscious, internalized convictions, you may resist new information that contradicts them because it poses a threat to your belief system. But if you cling to them, they become a self-fulfilling prophecy that leads to more rejection and abandonment, reinforcing the system. Unconscious coping strategies become excuses to avoid difficult aspects of life, thus crippling your emotional, interpersonal and spiritual development. Being closed-minded, skeptical, critical and judgmental of opposing new, more rational information only serves to create further separation and perpetuates disharmony. If left unaddressed, these outdated coping strategies will wreak havoc on your relationships, your health, and your happiness.

The quest for wholeness begins with honoring your inner truth, letting go of outlived beliefs, reassessing your interpretation of traumatic events, and developing more effective coping strategies. You must detach and heal from all the attachments, illusions, compulsions, fears and pain that complicate your journey. Abandon unhelpful illusions, self-images, attitudes, motives and irrational beliefs.

To do this, use detachment—the practice of letting go of everything that draws you away from your authentic self. When you let go of your old fears and pain, you are free to embrace your true self with compassion and love.

Detachment is about accessing a deeper, broader sense of your truest self, which is already whole and filled with the abundance of life, and allowing yourself to consider new information that may contradict your previous feelings and convictions. If you never risk looking outside your comfort zone, you limit achieving your potential and the joy and happiness you deserve to have. By allowing yourself to examine more rational information, you can reprogram your outdated, unrealistic beliefs. When you've done that, something magical happens—the gifts of self-knowledge, self-confidence and self-compassion are revealed.

Soulful Self-Reflection: Embracing Your True Self

When circumstances change abruptly, having a clear sense of self allows you to express your true thoughts and feelings with confidence and acknowledge your choices and desires with increased self-awareness. Grounded in a solid sense of personal autonomy, you are able to focus your attention and energy on gaining new insights and clarity about who you truly are and what is best for you at this new stage in life.

I invite you to spend some time embracing your true self to reveal any unrealistic, internalized beliefs or outdated coping strategies that may be negatively affecting your ability to live life more authentically.

Find a quiet place and settle yourself. Begin by sitting and breathing gently, inhaling long and deep and then exhaling in a slow and relaxed manner. Allow yourself to be led to the silence within.

Write your answers to the questions below that resonate strongly with you. Let your thoughts, feelings and insights flow without explanation or concern about proper grammar or spelling. Trust your inner voice as you consider these prompts:

- How effective am I at communicating my true thoughts and feelings, especially difficult or painful ones, like anger or hurt?
- Do I tend to deny or suppress my feelings or opinions, only to explode later over something unrelated?
- Do I conceal my true self to remain safe and secure?
- What must I do to practice honest, clear communication that strengthens and builds a deeper sense of my truest self?
- Is my life aligned with my beliefs, values, passions and purpose?

Pause now and reflect on what you discovered about how you want to live your life. Ask yourself what you might do to detach from unhealthy, internalized beliefs or self-sabotaging behaviors that keep

> you tied to the past. Identify one small step you will take to begin living more aligned with your true self.
>
> Adversities often reveal gifts of courage and confidence that may surprise or frighten you. The good news is that what you are searching for already lives within you—your true nature. Seeking inwardly with an open spirit brings you closer to knowing yourself and what you desire in life. Embracing your authentic self empowers you to face difficulties with increased self-reliance and bravery.

Healthy Boundaries

PERSONAL BOUNDARIES ARE THE GUIDELINES or limits you create to identify reasonable, safe and permissible ways of relating with others. Healthy boundaries allow us to discern our desires and needs in relationships and to set limits and advocate respectfully for ourselves when needed and appropriate. They encompass the physical, mental, emotional and spiritual realms, and collectively these boundaries make up the psychological container you use to define what is "you" and what is "not you."

With a clearly defined sense of self, you know who you are, which allows you to communicate your needs and desires effectively. Personal boundaries permit a separation between your own thoughts, feelings and needs, and those of others. They also teach you what you can control and what you can't. Responsibility and control are the stabilizing characteristics of healthy boundaries.

The "Serenity Prayer" encapsulates the fundamental premise of boundaries:

God grant me the serenity
to accept the things I cannot change,
the courage to change the things I can,
and the wisdom to know the difference.[17]

---

17 The "Serenity Prayer" was written by Reinhold Niebuhr in the 1930s. Alcoholics Anonymous began using a shorthand version of the "Serenity Prayer" in the twelve-step program and today it is one of the most well-known prayers.

It is healthy to set both external and internal boundaries. External boundaries have to do with your physical self and provide a sense of ownership and control over your physical being. They dictate how you react when someone violates your personal space and creates physical or emotional discomfort or a lack of safety. Your internal boundaries assist you with identifying your thoughts, feelings, actions, beliefs, choices and experiences; these are aspects you have personal responsibility and control over. With internal boundaries, you detach from the thoughts, feelings, actions, beliefs, choices and experiences of others; these aspects are outside your ability to control and are not your responsibility.

Having boundaries allows you to experience comfortable, safe interdependence with other people, resulting in mutually respectful, fulfilling relationships. With healthy boundaries, you can distinguish between acceptable and unacceptable behaviors and set limits for self-care when necessary and appropriate. They permit trust and security to develop and pave the way for achieving true intimacy where relationships can flourish. When boundaries are strong but flexible enough to allow self-discovery and mutual respect, you will enjoy opportunities to explore and develop your potential.

Personal boundaries require assertiveness, common sense, and good judgment. You must be willing to act on your own behalf instead of waiting to be rescued or blaming others for your problems. When you don't communicate your needs or assert your thoughts and feelings, your relationships will suffer. You can extract yourself from unhealthy situations or relationships and, hopefully, resolve difficulties if you speak up and use respectful and clear communication.

When you don't have healthy boundaries, you tend to lack a clear sense of self and derive your identity from other people. By allowing others to define you, you surrender who you are and may have difficulty making decisions in your own best interest. You may also believe your happiness and fulfillment lie elsewhere, with other people, things, places or experiences. Consequently, you may base your identity on temporary external manifestations of self-worth, such as your attractiveness, intelligence, achievements, wealth, popularity, prestige or material possessions—all of which can change and be lost at any moment.

Unhealthy boundaries emerge unconsciously as a consequence of growing up in households where there is no support to form a secure sense of self, to embrace emotional expression, to practice mutual respect, or to assert healthy boundaries. This environment may have consisted of too much harsh criticism, punishment or neglect. For some, their need for love and reassurance, coupled with a fear of abandonment and rejection, may cause them to be willing to do anything to prevent relationships from dissolving, resulting in an overwhelming need to take care of everybody and everything. Consequently, they may feel intense guilt when others are unhappy or when bad things happen. This can lead to a sense of unrealistic over-responsibility and a desire to control everything to maintain a false sense of safety and security. They may deny their own happiness and instead focus on the emotional and physical needs of others.

Learning to maintain healthy boundaries takes time, experience and regularly monitoring yourself. These limits involve a positive interplay between emotional attachment to others and the ability to maintain your self-care needs, which leads to a reciprocal flow of thoughts and feelings.

You can help delineate healthy boundaries, manage stress, and safely contain your emotional energy with intentional, conscious deep breathing. When a charged situation triggers an intense reaction, stop immediately and take a deep breath. Use your inhalation to ground yourself in the moment and your exhalation to release the tension. Grounding makes the integration of your thoughts, feelings, needs and desires possible. By focusing on your breathing, your negative internal dialogue will shut down, allowing you to focus on the present.

Clarity of thought and calm emotional control provide the basis for clear communication about what the problem is, how to solve it, and what is needed to restore balance to the relationship or stressful situation. To understand and control your thoughts and feelings, following these steps can be helpful:

1. Identify and name the problem.
2. Honestly clarify who is responsible.
3. Recognize your thoughts and feelings about the situation.
4. What, if anything, is within your control and your responsibility?

These simple steps allow clear communication for arriving at a mutually agreeable resolution.

Setting Clear Boundaries Exercise

If you feel overwhelmed when trying to set boundaries, use this simple and easy method. Imagine there is a horizontal line between your physical body and the other person or the stressful situation. This imaginary barrier is your boundary line. The space between it and your body is your responsibility and within your control. This includes your thoughts, feelings and behaviors in the present. The other side of the line represents the spatial area that is not your responsibility or within your control. This includes other people's thoughts, feelings and behaviors, as well as the past and future. Doing this exercise when you're feeling overwhelmed helps reestablish your autonomy and control, and detach from what you have no control or responsibility for.

When you practice healthy boundaries, clear communication, self-acceptance, and self-love, you can acknowledge and respect yourself and others more easily. You also have greater awareness of your thoughts and feelings, can ask for what you need, and act in your best interest. With the freedom to dance to your own rhythm, relationships develop and flourish, and there is greater appreciation for one another's uniqueness and beauty. Mature, healthy connections require profound self-acceptance and self-knowledge. When you recognize that your happiness is not dependent on others, you gain the confidence to meet your own needs while engaging in mutually respectful interpersonal relationships.

It may be helpful to contemplate the dynamics of your current relationships and whether they're healthy or not. If you discover you're trapped in unhealthy patterns, find ways to balance and heal your interactions with others.

Here are some things to consider:

- Allow others to make their own decisions and mistakes. Relinquish your efforts to control and manage the lives of other people, especially individuals who are capable of taking care of themselves. You cannot control and are not responsible for the happiness and personal growth of others.

- Learn to discriminate between pleasing and loving people; they are not necessarily the same. Loving others might involve pleasing them, but it also involves being true to yourself. It means respecting and valuing your own thoughts and feelings and expressing your needs and desires. While you might seek to please others as a strategy to

avoid conflict, you are not being truly honest about your feelings, fears or desires. If you live your life to please others, you end up pleasing no one.
- Set strong but flexible boundaries and maintain healthy interactions where you can experience comfortable, honest and safe interdependence with people. Mutually respectful, fulfilling relationships flourish when there is a reciprocal flow of feelings, thoughts, desires and needs that permits trust and security to develop. Both people have to show up and be present for this to work.
- Learn to speak your truth. When you do not speak truthfully, the level of trust is diminished. Saying what you need to say with love and compassion is much better than leaving things unsaid. If one person stops participating or interacting, the whole relationship is threatened. Honest, clear, respectful communication allows you to move beyond old fears to develop a healthy belief system and foster truthful connections.

Once you've established positive patterns of relating to other people, you'll often discover a reservoir of time and energy for your own life. Sadly, events that demand your focus might actually represent issues that need your attention. When you commit to facing your problems, you may find the happiness and contentment you are seeking. Honoring and valuing yourself rather than seeking validation and self-worth from other people or external manifestations fosters enduring and intimate relationships.

Soulful Self-Reflection: Healing Your Relationships

The foundation for building mature, mutually respectful relationships starts with establishing a safe environment where you feel accepted, heard and recognized for your uniqueness. Creating lasting relations requires healthy boundaries that promote trust, stability and true intimacy. Meaningful connections flourish when limits are firm, yet flexible enough to allow personal autonomy that encourages self-discovery.

To heal your unhealthy relationship patterns, I have prepared the following exercise to help you identify ways you interact with others that may create disharmony and threaten your emotional stability.

Find a quiet place and settle yourself. Begin by sitting and breathing gently, inhaling long and deep and then exhaling in a slow and relaxed manner. Allow yourself to be led to the silence within.

Reflect on the questions below and write about the ones that resonate strongly with you. Let your thoughts, feelings and insights flow without explanation or concern about proper grammar or spelling. Trust your inner voice as you consider these prompts:

- Can I maintain effective and appropriate boundaries when necessary?
- What unconscious, unrealistic beliefs do I have that might be perpetuating unhealthy boundaries?
- Do I assume responsibility for things outside of my control and that aren't my concern? If so, why?
- Do I stay in relationships too long, trying to make them work when it's clear they don't? If so, why?
- Am I clinging to security when change is called for? If so, why?

What makes life fulfilling are the relationships we form along the way. The journey toward wholeness takes courage. Despite your fear of not being perfect, being rejected, or losing control, when you implement healthy boundaries, your emotional connections will be strengthened. When you risk putting your new skills into practice, you will delight in the joy transformation can bring. Give it a try. See what a difference healthy boundaries can make in your life.

Chapter 4
Hearing Your Inner Voice

Language is both a mystery and a miracle. With it, we can convey our thoughts to others and explore the universe. It is largely programmed by what we hear in our immediate environment. We communicate by being talked with, listened to, and allowed to share our own thoughts, feelings, questions and needs. Expressing ourselves through words—spoken or written—is how we gain insight, learn about ourselves, and practice clear communication. Through honest, open interactions, we learn to think and reason for ourselves, take responsibility for our decisions, and discover the power of our inner voice.

Not only do we use language to communicate with other people in our external world, we have a voice we use to express our thoughts in an auditory way within our head, like having a conversation with ourselves. We use our inner monologue to reflect on what we do, how and why we behave as we do, how we critique ourselves, and how we connect knowledge, ideas and concepts. We have inner dialogues to rehearse a speech, formulate a plan, resolve a problem, sort through choices, make a decision, or recall an event, just to name of few. Our inner voice encompasses all of our internal thoughts, including verbal, visual, emotional and symbolic, whether spoken aloud or not.

Most people are aware of their inner voice, although recognizing their inner dialogue might vary depending on individual experiences. For example, while trying to teach you proper manners, your parent may have said, "Children should be seen and not heard" or "If you can't say something nice, don't say anything."

Being young and dependent on your parent, you may have interpreted this to mean that your true thoughts and feelings were not important or might cause someone to be hurt. Consequently, you may have ignored, denied or shut down honest expressions of your thoughts and feelings. This may have caused you not to trust your inner voice and led you to look outside yourself for other people to tell you how you should think and feel.

This reluctance to communicate inhibits your ability to express your beliefs, desires or needs, and you may yield or comply with others out of fear of upsetting or displeasing someone else. When your self-expression is thwarted or suppressed, you are not fully present in your relationships, and the world sees only a facade of your true self. You must find the courage to free your inner voice from fear, guilt and shame, so you can express yourself with confidence and integrity.

If you grew up in a household where having negative emotions, especially anger or hurt, was labeled as impolite and unacceptable, you learned to suppress your true thoughts and feelings or hide behind a false countenance. If you cannot speak your truth without fear of ridicule or rejection, you may struggle with silencing your inner critic—the internal voice that constantly criticizes your thoughts, feelings and actions. It may be unrelenting in its goal to silence or tame your courage and prevent you from expressing your personal truths.

But if you lacked a safe environment when you were growing up, you may have difficulty listening to your inner truth. Rather than attempting to control your external environment, which is impossible, you learned to cope by focusing on what is reasonable and achievable, managing your inner environment, using one or many of a variety of coping mechanisms. In homes where the atmosphere was hostile due to constant arguing, yelling, nagging or criticizing, you may have learned to speak in half-truths or fabricate stories to avoid disapproval, criticism or blame.

Leaving things unsaid or obscuring the truth prevents clear communication and interferes with healthy, intimate relationships. It is unrealistic to expect others to understand your thoughts, feelings and needs telepathically. When you shut down or stifle honest dialogue, you relinquish responsibility for having your needs met. Later, you may wonder why you feel neglected or disregarded. These unhealthy coping strategies only create relationship problems.

On the other hand, you may find yourself constantly talking. Excessive speech controls conversations by making the speaker the center of attention, but it cuts off reciprocal communication and drains your energy. If you are constantly talking, you cannot listen to others to have a more balanced and respectful dialogue. Instead of listening, you may be trying to avoid hearing something you disagree with or find uncomfortable. However, incessant, aimless chatter distances you from having meaningful connections and conceals emotional vulnerability.

People who grow up in homes where traumatic life events were kept secret may also have difficulty, feel uncomfortable, or avoid talking about challenging things they have experienced. If you've been chastised for speaking about suicide, addiction, sexual abuse, incarceration or a similar traumatic circumstance, you may doubt or mistrust your intuition or question your perceptions of reality. For example, a young person may be reluctant to disclose suicidal thoughts or that they are being touched inappropriately due to fear of not being believed or punished. Secrets only cause more pain and suffering and can result in devastating consequences.

One of the unfortunate consequences of keeping secrets and not having the freedom to ask questions or receive honest information is that you are left with no coping skills for dealing with future turbulent experiences. This may result in overwhelming feelings of anxiety, loneliness and isolation. If you've been burdened with keeping family confidences, then you have likely learned to be vigilant about your words and body language. When you don't speak up, it may cause others to assume you lack empathy for those who are experiencing difficult transitions or traumatic events. In your relationships, your reluctance to speak freely and honestly may ultimately create distance, deception or more secrets that further erode or destroy them.

Traumatic life events create upheaval in your physical, emotional, mental and spiritual realms. To survive, adapt and function normally, you develop defense mechanisms that keep anxiety-provoking memories from your conscious awareness. These mechanisms are unconscious mental processes that keep memories and thoughts locked away.

Denial is a defense mechanism that involves ignoring or not acknowledging the reality of something that seems overwhelming or stressful, to avoid anxiety. It is often used in situations where we are unable to face the truth of what is happening. In the short-term, the coping mechanism of denial gives you time to accept and adjust following a devastating change. But if denial persists, it can perpetuate thoughts like: "It can't be that bad" or "I'll get over it." If you continue to deny the truth of the situation, it may lead to negative or destructive consequences and potentially interfere with taking effective action to handle the crisis. The prolonged use of denial prevents you from dealing with reality and stressful events in a healthy way.

Dissociation is another unconscious mental process where you compartmentalize traumatic events to avoid feeling overwhelming emotional distress. The brain's strategy of keeping anxiety-provoking incidents separate from your conscious awareness may help you survive the experience, but the repressed memories of the trauma do not disappear. You must expend a considerable amount of psychic energy to exclude these unacceptable feelings and thoughts from your conscious mind. Severe trauma can cause debilitating depression and paralyzing anxiety. These memories may continue to affect your behavior, impede your ability to trust yourself and others, and negatively impact your sense of self-worth and the formation of trusting and intimate relationships.

Terrifying experiences are encoded differently in the brain from ordinary events. The mind tries to block traumatic memories to protect you from the overwhelming distress you experienced. These repressed memories can be triggered by sights, sounds, smells and emotions later in life, causing you to feel as if the past event is happening right now. These stored images and recollections surface via flashbacks, recurrent nightmares, night terrors or intrusive, distressing thoughts and feelings—all symptoms of post-traumatic stress disorder.

Processing repressed trauma requires a combination of different interventions focused on the psychological, social and physical management of the stress. Talking with a therapist or another trained professional about life transitions and tumultuous events can provide the cognitive integration required for healing emotional suffering.[18]

Cognitive integration helps provide an accurate context by relegating traumatic memories to the past and increasing your understanding of the experience, thereby transforming the repressed memory into something you can

---

18 van der Kolk, *The Body Keeps the Score,* 191–192.

talk about. Although recollections of the traumatic events are still there and will always be a part of your life, the intensity of the emotions will lessen. Cognitive integration allows you to think more clearly, have more compassion for yourself, and builds your emotional strength.

Brain imaging research shows that these repressed memories are initially imprinted as sensations or feeling states, with little verbal representation. When you are experiencing a traumatic event, your Broca's area, the speech center of the brain, is deactivated, leaving you unable to put your thoughts and feelings into words.[19]

Eye Movement Desensitization and Reprocessing (EMDR) is a powerful therapeutic procedure that enables people to heal from trauma without having to talk about it. Developed by Francine Shapiro, an American psychologist and educator, EMDR has been extensively researched as an effective treatment for relieving anxiety, stress and trauma.[20] Studies have shown it helps consciously integrate and reinterpret traumatic events coherently, instead of experiencing sensations and images that are divorced from any context.[21]

EMDR works by stimulating both hemispheres of the brain through having the person follow an object with their eyes, while not moving their head. This helps in reprocessing traumatic memories. People observe their experiences internally, without having to describe them verbally. The rapid eye movement technique allows a radical reduction in emotional intensity (desensitization), while allowing the integration (cognitive restructuring) and reprocessing of the distressing event. This enables the brain to naturally process and heal the memories. The technique allows the mind/brain to rapidly access memories and images from the past and puts them into context or provides a different perspective.

Traumatic events leave deep scars and wounds that can remain throughout a lifetime. They cannot simply be fixed, denied or discarded. With effective professional therapeutic interventions, the emotional trauma likely will lessen

---

19 van der Kolk, *The Body Keeps the Score*, 182–184.

20 Francine Shapiro, *Eye Movement Desensitization and Reprocessing: Basic Principles, Protocols, and Procedures* (The Guilford Press, 1995).

21 Francine Shapiro and Margot Silk Forrest. *EMDR: The Breakthrough Therapy for Overcoming Anxiety, Stress, and Trauma* (Basic Books, 1997).

in severity and intensity over time, and you will find yourself on the path to healing. The gifts of resilience and courage are your constant companions on your journey.

 ## Soulful Self-Reflection: Hearing the Voice Inside the Beat

You cannot escape challenges in life. Being broken open repeatedly is a promise written into the contract of human existence. Certainly, the journey can get tiresome. When you are suffering, you may want to give up hope and give in to despair. The Sufi mystic poet Rumi speaks of the voices of faith and hope in one of his poems and encourages us to follow them instead:

> Thine is the triumph-tone of my heart;
> its echo thrills through sky and space.
> A voice within it whispers low
> "I know thou'rt faint—but rise! This is the way."[22]

A more modern translation by Coleman Barks refers to this as "the voice inside the beat."[23]

The wisdom of your inner voice is always available to you. If you try to block its flow, speak in half-truths or silence it, your soul will resort to speaking louder to gain your attention.

It may take time to clear away the grumbling to create the environment you desire—but it is vital you listen. Although you don't need perfect conditions, you do need to be honest and pay attention to what your soul tells you. Despite the grumblings, you must remember that something is gestating inside, and being quiet allows you to listen to the voice as it calls, "Be still! Come! This is the way!"

Use this exercise to explore your innermost thoughts and desires.

---

[22] Rumi, *Mathnawi*, trans. E. H. Whinfield (1887).

[23] Coleman Barks, trans., *The Essential Rumi* (HarperCollins Publishers Inc., 1995), 122.

Find a quiet place and settle yourself. Begin by sitting and breathing gently, inhaling long and deep and then exhaling in a slow and relaxed manner. Allow yourself to be led to the silence within.

Acknowledge and accept your soul's grumblings and concerns without judgment. Let your inner voice reveal its divine nature. Can you hear it saying: "This is the way to a life worthy of your passion and purpose?"

Reflect on the following questions:

- Do I ignore thoughts or events that come up because they are too painful to acknowledge?
- Are there things I feel resigned to and helpless to change, or have I stopped paying attention to them when they make me upset or uncomfortable?
- What prevents me from listening to my heart's desires?
- What can I do to connect to my inner voice and allow it to reveal my true nature and my life's passion and purpose?

Your lesson in this lifetime is to find and claim your one precious voice, so you can hear your true song. The full expression of life is influenced by the rhythm and tone of all your grumblings; every vibration is connected. To quote a Sufi adage: "Each person has a unique note in the universal symphony, no one else can strike yours except you."[24]

---

24 Neil Douglas-Klotz, *The Hidden Gospel: Decoding the Spiritual Message of the Aramaic Jesus* (The Theosophical Publishing House, 1999), 101.

Alexis's Transformational Choice

Here's how one courageous conversation led to my friend Alexis's pursuit of passion and purpose.

> When I was twenty-four and living in San Francisco, my mother, Nancy, was diagnosed with an aggressive form of intestinal cancer and given three months to live. She was fifty and had dedicated her adult life to raising my younger brother and me, while putting many of her own creative and career ambitions on hold.
>
> I went home to Iowa and took care of her in the final months of her life. During this time, we had long, emotional, important conversations about choices, regrets and what it meant for her to be coming to the end of her life so much earlier than she'd imagined. We discussed the goals we'd both accomplished, the dreams we'd ignored, and we talked (often) about how much I loved to make art, something she had always seen me immerse myself in, but that no one in our family had ever considered a "real" job option. Art was a hobby, an escape, and a way to play, but not the stuff of a lifelong career.
>
> Our conversations were both urgent and meandering at the same time. Through them, a kind of permission emerged, one in which the woman I loved most in the world let me know it was okay to make choices that didn't have guaranteed outcomes, and that I didn't have to follow a prescribed path to happiness. Like so many other people in their early twenties who were just coming out of college with debt and confusion, I didn't want to disappoint my parents by confessing that, in fact, I didn't really love the subject I had majored in (political science), and that my three years of working in the nonprofit sector did not feel like they were leading me to something fulfilling, even though everything was unfolding as I thought it should.

After saying the hardest and most painful goodbye, I went back to San Francisco, in shock and grief, and continued to work as a grant writer and project manager. By all objective measures, I had a great job doing work that had a meaningful impact on people's lives, and I told myself I should be grateful to have gainful employment even if something wasn't connecting or that I was going through the motions of what was expected of me. (By whom, it wasn't clear…) Each day, I tried to convince myself I would find the spark that would make the work feel more creative, more interesting, and less hollow, and that the heaviness I felt was all part of just having lost my mother so suddenly.

Months went by, most, generally sparkless. During one particularly bland and stressful span of days, I decided to go for a drive in Golden Gate Park during my lunch hour. An El Niño had just blown through, and several trees had come down in the park, leaving it deserted and chaotic. I drove up to a traffic barrier blocking the main thoroughfare to the Pacific and, struck by an impulse that was completely out of character, got out of my car, looked around to see no one, and moved the barricade enough to drive around it. I navigated downed trees and arrived at the ocean, which was surging and rough.

Standing in the wind, I felt myself make The Choice. I was not going to spend my life doing work I didn't care about or doing something just to meet a vague sense of obligation to anyone else's expectations.

I wanted to make art, to paint and draw and explore the recesses of my imagination—to create images that carried color and meaning and mystery. The existential math was clear to me in that moment. My mother had died at fifty, and I was now twenty-five. It was time to leave my "great job" and risk being an artist, even if I had no idea what that meant.

I gave notice the next morning, and no one was surprised. The program director came in the day after that with a full set of oil paints, a gift she'd received years ago but had barely touched.

That set off a chain of experiences, all driven by the fully felt conviction that I needed to be an artist, not as a hobby, not as something squeezed in, but as a vocation, as life's purpose lived. I started taking studio classes at four different community colleges and from a private instructor, volunteered as an art classroom assistant, and turned my bedroom into a workspace. I still needed an income and took temporary office jobs, but now it felt like those were on the periphery, while learning from experienced teachers and making art was the core of my focus.

Over five years of taking night and weekend classes in the Bay Area, I gained the equivalent of a bachelor's in fine arts. I then had the opportunity to travel to South Africa with my partner, where I taught art as a volunteer for two years. I returned to the United States and entered a top-ranked master's of fine arts program. One year later, after I graduated, I was offered a tenure-track position at a leading research university, not just to teach art, but to pursue my creative research in embodied mixed media drawing.

I've now shown my artwork in over eighty exhibitions around the world (with more on the horizon), published essays on drawing and perception, curated international exhibitions, taught all levels of drawing, been granted tenure at a flagship state university, and most vitally, I know without reservation that I love what I do. The pandemic has opened even more doors for ways to work virtually, and I now run drawing workshops that bring together artists from all over the world to create in an engaged community.

What drove that first monumental choice on the Pacific Coast, and has driven its expansion ever since, was the full-on confrontation with what it means to be aware of why we do what we do, and to not default to habit or a sense of predetermined expectation.

In 1994, my mother recognized how much I loved drawing and that it was something I'd talked myself into putting on the back burner in the name of fulfilling what I thought were the expectations of others. I am now one year older than my mother was when she died. I have fifty-one years of life to her fifty. That awareness shakes me in so many ways—bringing me deep gratitude and gentle sorrow at what could have been for her, and a fully felt and fierce determination to keep living in concert with what I value and care for.

With age, too, comes a realization that the risks I took when I was in my midtwenties were perhaps ill-advised. (I went for a long spell without health insurance and often had zero savings.) Making a transition in my fifties would not be as "cliff-jumping" of an event since I now have more strategic tools at my disposal, a larger network of colleagues and friends who can offer good advice, and trust in my own professional skill and acumen. My next transition will be to where I'm even more deeply connected to my sense of what will be both fulfilling and financially sustaining.

Not everyone was supportive when I took the leap. While many people celebrated me making a radical shift out of my office job and into the arts, and I received support and care from family, strangers and friends, my choices evoked hostility or dismissal from others (again, family, strangers and friends). I realized judgment from the latter didn't hurt as much as I'd feared. Ultimately, it didn't hurt at all because the more it happened, the more the pattern and dynamics of others' expectations were so clearly rendered that it made my own convictions feel that much more correct and solid.

My uncertainty was and is still eclipsed by a deep trust in the satisfaction I feel in studio work and in opening that creative process to others.

> Whenever I do feel doubt, I can come back to my first choice and feel the bedrock, the foundation upon which I continue to build.

Courageous Conversations Can Heal

SINCE THE EARLY DAYS OF human evolution, we have gathered together and shared our experiences. We recounted our dreams and visions, painted images on rocks to share with others, told stories about our days, and felt comforted by the presence of those closest to us. Today, we live in a very noisy environment, constantly bombarded by sounds and technology. We move at a frantic pace into greater isolation and fragmentation. People are clamoring for attention and connection, yet the simple act of sitting face-to-face and conversing is becoming obsolete. We all need time together, to listen, to dream, to support, and to reconnect.

Human conversation is the most ancient and easiest way to cultivate the conditions for change on all levels: personal, relational, communal, organizational and global. Simple dialogue gives us each a chance to speak, to feel heard, and to listen to one another. If we can sit together and talk about what is important to us, we come alive with one another. Having open discourse takes time, patience and a willingness to speak about our heartfelt truths with purpose and intention. Honest conversation moves us closer to a hopeful future.

In the English language, the word for *health* comes from the same root as the word for *whole*. And *whole* is derived from the same root word as *holy*. Conversation moves us closer to one another. It helps us become more *whole*, more *healthy*, and more *holy*. If we are willing to meet face-to-face, listen attentively, and honestly speak our deepest truths, we might just weave the world into *wholeness* and *holiness*.

One of the simplest acts of human kindness is also the most healing. Merely listening to someone, not advising or coaching, but silently and fully listening, is a healing gift. Science has shown that nothing in the universe exists as an isolated or independent entity; everything takes form in relationship to something else. Our natural state is to be in community, and despite all the technological advances society has made, we have never lost our need to connect. Listening is the essence of all successful relationships, including familial, collegial, professional, romantic, social and global.

We foster clear communication through attentive listening. In the book *The Circle Way*,[25] authors Christina Baldwin and Ann Linnea describe attentive listening as the practice of sitting quietly, with compassion and patience, and listening closely, without speaking, to truly hear the other person. This allows you to hear their thoughts, feelings and stories while staying separate.

Many times during a conversation, we are in our own heads, just waiting for our turn to interject our thoughts and stories with problem-solving or advice. Other times, we take things personally, internalize them, prejudge the situation, or defend ourselves rather than truly listening to what is being communicated. We may not agree with the person, like their story, or even like the person telling the story, but listening brings us closer to one another. By remaining curious, you can seek a place of connection even when there is disagreement. Attentive listening is a spiritual practice that shifts you out of reactivity and into deeper inquiry with others.

Intentional speaking is the flip side of attentive listening. It is the practice of contributing our own relevant stories, thoughts, feelings or information to the conversation.[26] It enables us to slow down, breathe and be present, and wait patiently for the moment when we understand what we want to add to the conversation. Intentional speaking does not mean automatically agreeing with others, but rather sharing our truth. It means considering the impact of our words and actions before, during and after we talk, and offering our contribution in a way that will benefit the conversation and the relationship. When we speak with purpose and intention, we are filled with an abiding faith in the wisdom of each person to know their own truth.

We all have a story, and all of us want to tell it to feel validated and honored. With attentive listening and intentional speaking, you can communicate from your heart, knowing your words will be received without judgment or criticism. Whatever you have experienced, if you can tell your story and know you have

---

25 Christina Baldwin and Anan Linnea, *The Circle Way: A Leader in Every Chair* (Berrett-Koehler Publisher, Inc., 2010), 27.

26 Baldwin and Linnea, *The Circle Way*, 28.

been heard, you will find it easier to deal with life's difficulties. If no one listens, you can end up repeating your story to yourself, which can eventually keep you stuck. Now is the time to commit to sharing your truth.

Soulful Self-Reflection: Starting Courageous Conversations

Have you ever wondered what it would feel like to have a simple, honest conversation where we each could speak our truth, feel heard, and attentively listen with mutual respect and curiosity? A common lament of our time is often that "no one really sees me, hears me, or understands me."

Having a courageous conversation invites you to experience the joy of an honest and heartfelt dialogue designed to develop the necessary skills for building meaningful and healthy relationships. Being present, listening attentively, and speaking your innermost truth are practices you can learn that will enhance the well-being of your interactions. Simply to be seen and heard is the healing gift your soul longs for.

Is there someone you'd like to deepen your relationship with? The following structured dialogue is designed to allow you to experience a courageous conversation using the skills that build healthy interpersonal relationships.

> In this exercise, find another person or two with whom you'd like to practice having a courageous conversation. When you meet with them, turn off all devices that keep you attached to the multitasking world.
>
> Set an intention for your conversation. Agree on a time frame and format: how long each person will talk, who will begin, and how it will end. While one person is speaking, the others agree to listen attentively.
>
> Begin by sitting and breathing gently for a few moments to become calm and centered. Allow everyone enough time to gather their thoughts so each person can speak with purpose and intention. Respect and trust the process.

Select a mutually acceptable topic or question from those listed below or formulate your own to explore:

- When was the last time I reflected on something important to me?
- When in my life have I experienced clear, honest communication?
- What is my unique contribution to the world?
- When have I experienced healing that changed my life?

Once you've agreed upon the topic, the first person can begin. As a listener, try to stay focused on what the speaker is saying. As responses come to mind, let them pass by just as easily as they came. Continue listening purposefully to what the speaker has to share.

When it is your turn, be mindful that this is the time to share your truth. So, be honest about your feelings. Stay focused on the topic, but also remain respectful toward those who are listening. Address any issues that were brought up by those who spoke before you, in order to share your viewpoint and move the conversation in a positive direction.

Each of us is on a quest to discover our truth, to learn how to listen to our inner voice, and to discover our unique path. Attentive listening and intentional speaking are gifts we give to one another that help us along this journey. Knowing we can share what we hope to say and listening to what others have to contribute cultivates lasting relationships, sustained by mutual respect and dignity.

Chapter 5
Trusting the Unfolding

Transitions are not convenient or easy. You may feel lost as you step into the unknown, where there are no road signs with arrows to reassure you that "This is the way!" The familiar rules don't seem to apply anymore. While you may not feel like your "old" self, your "new" self is not yet fully formed. It is risky to feel so vulnerable. Letting go of a known situation that promised security, but now challenges you to move into unknown territory, can create apprehension and anxiety. You must undergo a transformational process to come to terms with your past and surrender to how life unfolds.

The abrupt and unexpected nature of endings can leave you feeling as if things are chaotic and out of control. They force you to readjust your priorities, relinquish old and outlived patterns of relating, and go in search of new opportunities that nourish your mind, body and spirit. But transformation can only take place if you let go of your old assumptions about how life "should" be.

This process may seem more like a tug of war than a surrender. We may feel a compelling need to cling to the past and often yearn for the predictability and false sense of control we had in the "good old days" when everything was familiar. In actuality, things may not have been so good, and control was only an illusion. We may hang on to the past because we cannot bear the uncertainty and unpredictability change brings. In these cases, sometimes it takes a crisis to remind us we are not in control. The worst has already happened, and we are holding on to a time that no longer exists. The truth is that we may be clinging to things that are no longer of real importance or necessary to our current circumstances.

There comes a time when things that were undoubtedly good and right for you must be left behind. Allow space to grieve what has been lost. The seductive influence of safety and the false promises that life will always remain the same must be examined. Slow down and take stock of what doesn't work anymore.

Letting go of the past is the only way for something new to take root. Release is the precursor to being reborn. Life asks us to surrender the past and reinvent ourselves every time we confront change. When you leave space for new beginnings, you experience the rare and precious opportunity to learn more about yourself.

To better understand why endings are part of the necessary and natural rhythm of transitions, you must learn to see life as a series of cycles: growth, maturation, death and rebirth. Beginnings require letting go of old, outlived beliefs and dreams to make room for new growth, goals and desires in your next phase of life. Just as old tree branches that no longer bear fruit must be pruned to allow new growth, our old roles, relationships, activities and ambitions must be reexamined, reprogrammed and relinquished for our inner truth to come to the forefront. A pruned tree may not look beautiful at first, but by harvest time it yields an abundance of lovely new fruit.

When you trust the promise that something bountiful is yet to come, you gain a sturdier, more resilient faith in life. Pruning strengthens rather than diminishes what is there, allowing you space to mature and flourish. It may be time to put dead things to rest, whether that be a dream, a relationship, or a "false" self, so new life can ripen and come into being.

The transformational journey is the process of surrendering to a time of great difficulty. This involves shedding whatever we carry that has outlived its purpose and is no longer alive or meaningful. That means leaving behind an outdated lifestyle to move forward, discarding an old way of relating that has become suffocating, or casting off irrational beliefs about people and the world that hold you captive to the past. You must surrender your self-destructive beliefs and patterns of relating to others so you can birth new ones that align with the truths of your authentic self.

When you surrender the old, you are reborn in the present, where you are free to become your truest self. You do not have to wait until you are on your deathbed to discover who you truly are. You only need to let go of your past through life's mini-deaths, your journey of endings and beginnings. When you come to terms with your past and prune away what no longer serves you, a new vision can be born.

Soulful Self-Reflection: Trusting Spirit's Pruning Hand

We all need pruning to expand in new directions and fertile soil to replenish our spirits. Just as dead fruit or fallen leaves produce springtime renewal, our broken dreams and painful endings become the rich environment where new visions can ripen and joyful relationships can flourish. Pruning is a process of purification, allowing life's bountiful gifts to manifest. Your greatest challenge is to recognize your spirit's pruning hand and to trust that the sweetness of life will be tasted anew.

It may be the right time to:

- prune what no longer serves you or brings joy and meaning to your life.
- gently loosen space around your soul and weed out your outlived roles, unnecessary activities, nonessential ambitions, and unrealistic illusions.
- connect with what sparks your imagination and quickens your pulse.
- consider what still serves you in this season of your life and what you can do away with to make room for something new.

Let me share a meditation with you that will enable you to identify aspects of your life that may no longer bring meaning or excitement for you today, and then commit to a new goal, dream or vision that would bring passion and purpose to your life.

Find a quiet place and settle yourself. Begin by sitting and breathing gently, inhaling long and deep and then exhaling in a slow and relaxed manner. Allow yourself to be led to the silence within.

Reflect on the following questions:

- Am I still dreaming, or have I given up and settled for comfort and familiarity?
- What are my dreams at this new season of my life?
- What needs pruning that no longer brings me joy and meaning?
- Is there a new vision that sparks my imagination that would allow me to expand and flourish to my full potential?
- What could I commit to today that would move me closer to a new vision worthy of my passion and purpose?

Once you're done, decide what you plan to do with these new insights at this season of renewal.

When you practice healthy boundaries, cultivate your inner voice, engage in courageous conversations, and claim your authentic self, you will discover new ways of relating to others that replenish your spirit and nourish your soul. Relinquishing old, unhealthy patterns and redefining more realistic beliefs about yourself and your place in the world will restore your emotional balance and heal your wounds. As you learn to accept your losses and face adversity, you will gain wisdom that aids in your healing.

Transitions demand that you find courage and deep trust that whatever is unfolding carries the possibilities of new beginnings. The Dalai Lama instructs, "We can never obtain peace in the outer world until we make peace with ourselves." Until you are tested to the point of thinking you may not survive, until you stop resisting and face adversity, you cannot fully understand your personal power and courage. Change and loss can still jerk the rug out from beneath you, but when you discover you are resilient and resourceful, you can dust off the debris and move forward amid life's hardships, stronger and more confident than ever. Befriending your pain will lead you to imagine a new vision beyond immediate endings where all that has unfolded is not lost.

Transformation becomes possible once you are willing to search inwardly for deep meaning and wisdom. When you become conscious of how you view change, you gain the confidence and resilience to approach future endings with greater courage and hope. With this new strength, you make decisions for a more purposeful and meaningful life. As you incorporate this new frame of reference into your mindset, transitions can become exciting opportunities to bravely relinquish the past and move forward with an open heart and mind to create the life you desire. When you let go of the past and trust the hope inherent in new beginnings, a vision for the future will unfold, bringing joy and gratitude with it.

Chapter 6
Bridging Endings to New Beginnings

Transitions can shake your sense of stability. They test your strength and force you to adapt in ways you never expected. But even the hardest moments can give your life new purpose and meaning. When you learn to accept this ongoing cycle of change, you make space for hope—and faith in a brighter tomorrow.

The medieval Italian poet Dante Alighieri wrote in his majestic poem, *Divina Commedia*:[27]

> In the middle of the journey of our life I found myself in a dark wood where the straight way had been lost sight of.

It's not uncommon to find yourself periodically feeling as though you are in a dark wood, having lost your way. No amount of forethought, good intentions, or advice can spare you from periods of confusion, disappointment and dissolution when life suddenly changes and you are confronted with the reality of the continuous cycle of endings and beginnings.

During your lifetime, you will navigate through many transitions—each one contributing to your personal growth and inner transformation. Experiencing births, weddings and deaths makes you realize sadness and joy are never truly

---

27 Dante Alighieri, *The Divine Comedy of Dante Alighieri*, trans. Dorothy L. Sayers (Penguin Books, 1949).

separate. When you celebrate the birth of a new life, you must contemplate eventually letting them go as well. While mourning the death of a loved one, you must also give thanks for a life well lived. There can be tears at weddings and laughter at funerals. The art of living wisely is accepting the reality that, just as endings and beginnings are interconnected, so too are the past and the future. As you consciously grasp this idea, you learn to let go of the past and surrender to how life unfolds. By honoring this truth, you are able to appreciate and be grateful for these moments.

Life is a succession of thresholds to be crossed. A threshold is not a simple boundary; it is a space that divides familiar territory from a frontier yet to be discovered. When you have left one phase in life but have not yet entered the next, you are betwixt and between. You are the most teachable in this middle space because you are vulnerable. Thresholds embody the tension between who we are and who we can become. The space between endings and beginnings is where the arduous work of gleaning wisdom from our experiences occurs.

Like all of us, I'm sure you would prefer that your world would remain stable and predictable, but this expectation is neither reasonable nor realistic. The challenge is to stop trying to make everything happen according to your preconceived plan of how life "should" be or how you "expect" it to be. Instead of demanding answers to all your questions—"Why is this happening? How can I get through this dark place? What am I to do now?"—trust that when something ends, a space will open. Let go of your need to fix, control or even fully understand why something is happening. Slow down and notice what is right in front of you and what you might miss seeing in your futile attempt to run away from the pain of change. If you live completely on the surface, you miss out on the wisdom adversities can teach you.

Transitions unravel your sense of safety and security. Whenever something changes in your external world, either positive or negative, you experience a shift in your internal world as well. This may ignite the feeling that you do not know who you truly are, why you are alive, or how you want to spend your limited and precious time on earth. All adversity has the potential to reveal your wisdom.

When challenges occur, you must bravely ask yourself:

- How do I embrace change when things fall apart?
- What is this transition teaching me about myself and my purpose?

When you're suspended between the past and the future, it can be confusing and intense as you grieve your losses and sort through your options as you search for a new vision. As you come to terms with the painful endings in your life, you have to establish a whole new set of roles and goals for yourself.

Your inner compass helps you create a new framework for your life. This becomes a time to identify, reexamine and reprogram beliefs and values you've outlived and relinquish stifling routines and roles that keep you tied to the past. Transitions provide unique opportunities to reclaim forgotten dreams, set different goals, and create a new vision. As you gain a fresh perspective on your painful circumstances, you can turn your struggles into a wiser, more resilient, and passionate vision for the future. If you befriend endings and awaken the wisdom that dwells deep within your soul, you'll discover that surprises and unpredictability serve as keys to spiritual growth and transformation.

Transitions teach you the hard lesson that when something changes or ends in your life, a path will ultimately open to a new vision. In the book *Four Quartets*, renowned poet T. S. Eliot wrote about what is true of all transitions:

> What we call a beginning is often an end. And to make an end is to make a beginning.[28]

Endings leave behind a hollow space that becomes an opening for new adventures, dreams and visions for the future. Accepting this fact helps sustain your hope amid chaos and confusion.

Entering into new territory may feel perilous and threatening. When you're just trying to stay afloat, it can feel impossible to see the shore. The challenge is not to escape the pain of change, nor do you want to let yourself drown in it. Instead, gather your courage to enter those turbulent waters and risk being immersed in darkness. Your task is to trust that life will unfold as it should while you search inwardly for hope and meaning in a new beginning.

Everything that happens is part of your journey. All of your experiences are meant to teach you who you are and what gives your life purpose and meaning. Your thoughts and feelings must be acknowledged and attended to in order to gain wisdom. It is important to feel what you feel and go through it all. When you

---

28 T. S. Eliot, "Little Gidding" in *The Four Quartets* (Harcourt Brace & Company, 1971), 58.

allow time for things to unfold organically and wait patiently, you'll discover the lesson in each transition and be able to make your life easier in the future.

Elizabeth's Revelations from the Soul

Here is a story of how listening to one's intuition and instincts helped guide my friend Elizabeth's choices to create a more balanced and meaningful life.

> I was lucky to have the chance to attend college, but I was totally clueless when I arrived on campus. My father chose a school and major for me—one that was suitable for an "independent woman"—possibly because my mother was financially dependent, had not finished high school, and did not work outside the home. I enrolled as an accounting major at my dad's alma mater, which made him proud. He was footing the bill, so I didn't argue.
>
> My first epiphany came during my junior year. I was in the dorm cafeteria studying financial accounting standards from a huge textbook. This was my first hardcore accounting class. I remember staring at a single page for several hours, reading the same paragraph over and over, as if I had a reading disability. I couldn't focus on the words or understand anything, sort of like reading a foreign language without a dictionary. My eyes just glazed over. With absolute certainty, I knew accounting was not for me: I could not and would not continue down this path.
>
> It was the first time I'd had a physical reaction and paradigm shift that led to a life transition. I couldn't focus on the book no matter how much I tried because I couldn't see myself in this vocation. A few days later, I dropped my business classes, found a part-time job, and informed my father that I was done with accounting. It did not go well, and my source of parental financial aid ended. I was on my own. It would be almost nine years before I held a "real job," according to my father's standards. In the meantime, I transferred into the biology department.

I continued to frustrate my family as I worked my way through college and postgraduate studies. I was living well below the poverty line and had large student loans. My family had no frame of reference for my life as a graduate student, which is essentially slave labor at the lab bench. But I had found my passion—solving problems in biology gave me energy and consumed my analytical brain in a way that accounting could not. Proving hypotheses and publishing findings was an unbelievable high. Within a few years of my appointment to an academic position, I had created a strong research program and started pulling in grant money. My drive and passion paid off, and my father forgave me for walking out of accounting class.

My life in academia worked for many years—until I hit a wall. A mixture of grief after my divorce, a loss of collegiality in the workplace, and a nagging feeling that "work was not working" became my new norm. Unexpectedly, I had a big awakening on a routine drive to campus for a meeting. I found myself unable to get out of the car and walk into my building. There was nothing wrong with the entrance, and there were plenty of parking spaces, but I couldn't make myself go inside. It was strange. I kept circling the building and reparking, then pulling out to drive around and repeat the process. This was accompanied by a sense of loss and an epic amount of tears and frustration.

Eventually, I was pulled over by campus police and questioned. I told the cop I was lost and didn't know where I belonged anymore. Once again, I was in the midst of a shift, and the physical and mental manifestations couldn't be ignored. I was grieving for a reason, and an ending was looming on the horizon.

Since I was too young to stop working, I needed a plan. I explored options for changing jobs, moving to another university, and applying for a post in administration. These were valid options, but as I visualized them, I could feel my energy wane. Deep inside, I knew these choices weren't right for me. And I wasn't going to fake my way into a situation that didn't feed my soul. Without a strong commitment, it is almost impossible to navigate the hard times.

Although science was my career, I had recently developed an interest in yoga and had started teaching classes as a side gig. After a few months of leading sessions, I realized my soft yoga voice was calming to others. I had a growing group of participants, and based on that, I decided to continue teaching yoga after I left my faculty position. My colleagues thought I was crazy. However, after years of living mostly in my analytical left brain, I was seeking balance. Every time I stood in front of a yoga class, I would watch the group, get a sense of what they needed, and then dive right into the sequence, using verbal cues and my body. It was so very different from teaching technical material in a classroom.

I slowly let go of my academic role and allowed others to see me simply as a yoga instructor, which was challenging. I was shedding my academic identity and transitioning into a new role my peers viewed as less prestigious.

It is extremely difficult to make a living teaching yoga, and I never assumed it would be a primary income source. Thankfully, I still had a deep love of science and a passion for helping others, so I started to freelance as a science editor/writer and formed my own consulting business.

As I planned my exit, I worked simultaneously as a professor, yoga instructor, freelance writer, and consultant. Although the days were long and I had a lot on my plate, I wanted a soft landing as I parachuted out of academia and into gig work. To prepare for the impending loss of steady income, I practiced living on a very small portion of my salary. This was possible because I was single with no children. However, it was daunting because my divorce had left me with no savings, and now I needed a financial cushion.

As I transitioned out of my stable position, I developed new hobbies, and several became income streams and side gigs. My job in academia had imparted many transferable skills. I was used to hunting for opportunities, solving problems, troubleshooting and talking to large groups of people. My proficiency in these areas served me well after I left my tenured faculty position.

The take-home message from my story is to listen to your intuition and instincts. They are truly gifts. The two transitions I described above were both accompanied by physical symptoms and mental stress. We all receive signals from our environment, and most do not compel us to make big decisions. However, some signs literally beg for attention and keep reappearing until we listen and receive the message.

Although the process of radical transformation is uncomfortable and unsettling, I'm grateful my instincts continue to guide me down the winding road of big changes. Everything is temporary, including the discomfort of transition. It is a courageous act to listen to our intuition, move forward, step into the "unknown," and journey to the other side.

Your Intuitive Self

WHENEVER YOU'RE GOING THROUGH A time of change, it is helpful to search inward with an inquisitive spirit to find your intuitive self. This is the source of insights, dreams and synchronicities. These are not mere impulses that help you through life's struggles. They also serve as signals that something new and exciting is coming. When you learn to trust your intuitive self, you free your natural courage and ability to cast out fear, opening up your life to new thresholds of discovery, creativity and compassion. When you allow your intuitive self to guide your choices, you gain clarity and meaning.

It is also helpful to reflect on both your inner experiences (insights, dreams and intuitions) and the gifts you receive from the outer world (synchronicities), which are the ordinary events in your life. If you look for patterns in common occurrences, you start to see their significance and appreciate what they have to teach you. The insights they provide increase the probability that you will continue on your true path. Everything that happens is a form of feedback. Interpreting it properly is critical to understanding how you should proceed on your life journey. When you create a firm foundation that supports your insights, dreams, synchronicities and intuitions, you gain happiness and peace of mind.

Self-reflection involves introspection. This is the realm of intuition, knowledge and wisdom. Introspection turns your attention from your exterior world to your interior world: your private emotions, insights, intuitions, wishes and desires. Your subconscious and unconscious processes are directly linked to what you think, feel and experience. Becoming more aware of these thoughts and emotions improves your ability to respond productively, creatively and adaptively to crises throughout your lifetime.

When you adopt an attitude of curiosity and introspection with even the most mundane routines, you see the people and circumstances of your life with fresh eyes. You can recognize the bigger picture without illusion or distraction. When you unlock your intuition, you begin to discern meaningful patterns, insights and dreams. By creating your own unique rhythm between your conscious and unconscious worlds, your mind becomes focused, your intuition is enhanced, and you gain clarity about your authentic self and purpose.

Although some individuals seem naturally endowed with strong intuitive powers, it can be a learned skill. Practicing is best accomplished the scientific way: through trial and error, testing and observing. In his book *The Intuitive Edge*, Philip Goldberg suggests acting on impulse as a way to practice intuition.[29] Try using it by making quick decisions on minor matters, like bringing an umbrella on a sunny day, leaving earlier than planned for a meeting, or choosing a book at random. Start with simple things. Look for repetitive patterns. Keep a record of your hunches and see how often they are accurate. If you're feeling compelled to accept an invitation, make a move or stay put—try it out and document the

---

29 Philip Goldberg, *The Intuitive Edge: Understanding and Developing Intuition* (J. P. Tarcher, 1983).

outcome. Over time and with practice, you'll begin to recognize and trust your gut feelings, which is a step toward accessing your intuitive self.

While you're nurturing your skill, start each morning with the expectation that the events of the day may contain a clandestine message addressed to you personally. Expect omens, epiphanies, casual blessings, and teachers who will unknowingly speak to your situation. These encounters might include:

- a casual comment from a friend that provides insight and direction for your life
- an offer to collaborate on a project that takes you in a new direction
- the loss of a job that pushes you toward the career you had visualized for years
- an illness or accident that reminds you of what is really important in life
- a sudden crisis that calls forth strengths you never realized you possessed

At some point, the mysterious lamp of intuition begins to shine through where linear thought does not. Even the most gifted scientists follow their intuition. Regardless of how many experiments they perform in the lab or how many hypotheses they put on paper, there comes a point where they take a leap of faith based on informed intuition. On this journey toward self-discovery, we are all scientists, and our life is the laboratory.

Most spiritual traditions regard dreams as revelations from the soul. Whether a dream comes when you are awake or asleep, it reveals information that remains invisible in the broad daylight of consciousness. They beckon you in directions you might need to travel to achieve personal growth, integration of your consciousnesses, and relational health. They reveal your true feelings about things you may be pondering. Dreams help you refine your direction and reevaluate your vision for the future. The insights they disclose may relate to unfinished business or help validate that you are on the right path. They remind you that your life is larger than your conscious experiences and point you toward balance and wholeness.

Psychiatrist Carl Jung posited that we dream continuously, even during waking hours, drawing on material from the unconscious mind. However, our conscious minds may obscure its message.[30] Dreams provide information from

---

30 Carl G. Jung, *Memories, Dreams, Reflections* (Vintage Books, 1963).

your unconscious about current real-life struggles that require your attention. If you ignore what they're trying to tell you, you will dream about them repeatedly until you pay attention. As with anything you attempt to deny or avoid, the more you try to block out your dreams, the more likely it is that the message will affect other parts of your life in the form of anxiety, confusion or even illness.

After my divorce, I experienced a recurring dream where I frantically climbed up and down the bleachers of a gigantic stadium, desperately searching for my lost purse, which contained my driver's license, money, keys and other personal items. Obviously, my recurring dream metaphorically symbolized my questions about "Who am I now?" and "How can I create stability after this major crisis?" Ironically, as I began reevaluating my life's course and formulating a new vision for my future, the dream stopped its nightly visitations.

The heart of dream work is deciphering the messages they bring. Listening to them is an act of humility. They are windows into your creative life. When you remember your dreams, you usually feel more inspired, intuitive and receptive to messages from your subconscious. Giving dreams your attention, granting them autonomy and mystery, goes a long way toward discovering the wisdom they offer.

Contrary to what we may think, everyone dreams, and we typically have half a dozen of them per night. We may not want to remember our dreams because of the messages they contain, the things they reveal, and the directions they give us. Our ability to remember them is largely shaped by how much attention we pay to them. They respond not only to our attention but also to direct requests.

Here are a few tips to capture the messages in your nighttime dreams:

1. Get in the habit of asking for dream guidance before you fall asleep. Keep a journal and pen by your bedside. When you request a dream, be specific. For example, ask for directions about how to resolve a problem, for clarification of another dream, etc.
2. Immediately upon awakening, write down your dreams before your feet hit the floor. Becoming fully awake can deplete your memory of the dream and reduce its impact and energy.
3. As you journal, brainstorm all the associations you can think of between the visions or events in your dreams, especially the most potent emotions or images. Which words, ideas, people, memories or feelings does the dream remind you of? Go with the connection that elicits the

most energy. Remember that dreams are subjective and relate to things happening in your daily life. What is the dream trying to tell you? Do images in it symbolize events in your life?

Synchronicities are events that seem related but are not explained by conventional causality. Jung believed synchronicities mirror deep psychological processes that carry messages in the same way dreams do. They take on meaning and provide guidance in our inner world through our thoughts, feelings, visions, dreams and premonitions.[31]

Synchronicities happen with regularity, although we rarely notice them until they become explicit. They primarily communicate with you through your intuition, providing signals that indicate an appropriate course of action. Synchronicities are clues that point to a higher vision or bigger picture than you might ever have imagined.

Meditation and synchronicities are connected; the more you meditate, the more synchronicities you will experience. In their insightful book *Synchronicity*, Allan Combs and Mark Holland write that both engage activities in a zone between consciousness and unconsciousness where messages from our soul are delivered.[32] Synchronicities remind you to pay attention to your life. Most importantly, they bring astonishment, which helps you reconnect with the miracle and awe of life, while recognizing them helps you gain insight for your journey toward wholeness.

Your soul will do what is necessary to keep you on your spiritual path. When you trust your intuitive self during times of change, you begin to believe that life will unfold as it should, and that a brighter vision can emerge even from the darkness. By releasing your limiting beliefs, you align more closely with your true self and move toward your higher purpose. Even as your circumstances continue to evolve, you will learn to adapt in ways that nurture wholeness. Devoting time to listen consciously to your inner voice deepens your trust in its wisdom, creating new opportunities for a more purposeful and meaningful life.

---

31 Jung, *Memories, Dreams, Reflections*.

32 Allan Combs and Mark Holland, *Synchronicity: Through The Eyes of Science, Myth, and the Trickster*, 3rd ed. (Grand Central Publishing, 2001).

The Need for Silence

THE UNCERTAINTY AND BUSYNESS OF a hectic life can pull you away from being in touch with your innermost being. Oftentimes, you may find yourself living too fast, never still, never quiet, always rushing to the next activity, hurrying to meet someone else's expectations, or taking care of an obligation that may not even be yours or something you enjoy. You risk losing your true self when you become distracted by what the world tells you about who you are, depend on other's opinions about how you are expected to be, allow others to use you for their purposes, or strive to conform to their demands.[33]

Silence and solitude can help you release your fears and reconnect with your true self. Being quiet and alone provides space for you to let go of the noise of your busy life and withdraw from distractions and conversations. This, in turn, allows you the time and space to listen to the soft stirrings of your soul that call: "Come, rest. Replenish your spirit in a place of unceasing love and acceptance. Be gentle with yourself. Let love and peace surround and comfort you."

We all need periods of respite. Searching inward with an inquisitive spirit requires the self-discipline to resist the urge to look elsewhere for answers to your problems, concerns and questions. Without quiet, introspective moments, you lose your grounding and become distracted by the many demands for constant attention.

Solitude and silence help you find the courage to go deep into the desert of your pain and suffering. When you practice this inward seeking, you become more comfortable with the stirrings of your soul.[34] At first, your attention may constantly be interrupted by your "monkey mind," which will attempt to distract you with persistent thoughts. Slowly, with tenacity, you will discover a calm, familiar inner landscape that deepens your longing to remain "at home" with yourself.[35]

---

33 Henri J. M. Nouwen, *You Are the Beloved: Daily Meditations For Spiritual Living* (Convergent Books. 2017), 20.

34 Nouwen, *You Are the Beloved*, 52.

35 Pema Chödrön, *How To Meditate: A Practical Guide to Making Friends With Your Mind* (Sounds True, 2013), 61–62.

When you no longer fear getting to know yourself and can focus your attention on your inner stirrings, you begin to experience the joy of unconditional love and compassion. Deep silence and solitude lead you to accept and be compassionate toward yourself. Becoming calm in quiet moments encourages your creative energy to flow with abundance to light your path.

Self-nurturing rituals, which honor silence and solitude, will help keep your life well-balanced—physically, mentally and spiritually. Quiet rituals replenish your energy, which can be easily depleted with daily demands and pressures. Make sure you regularly schedule time to be alone to collect your thoughts and restore your soul. Set boundaries around your accessibility; let go of responsibilities and be unavailable to the rest of the world, even if it is just for a few moments.

Creating a Sacred Refuge

Solitude and silence are needed to tune into your heart, the place where you can listen for that clear, soft voice that whispers from the center of your being. It is there that you can discover the source of your loneliness and face your fears, the place you go to hear the truth.

Without regular moments of silence and solitude, your creative energy will be drained, leaving you depleted and diminished. To find nourishing rest for your body, mind and soul, it is crucial to create a space where you can withdraw from your hectic life and go inward to listen for the still, small voice inside.

Let me share a simple and practical way for you to create a sacred refuge, where you can find the solitude and silence needed to restore your physical, emotional and spiritual energy.

Find a quiet space where you can shut the door to the outside world, withdraw in solitude, and just "be." Select a chair or couch big enough to nestle into and feel supported, and place it there for you to relax into.

You may want a small table near you to hold objects infused with happy memories: a rock carried home from a family trip to the mountains, the hand-painted teacup that belonged to your grandmother, photos of loved ones and friends celebrating joyful moments… These simple objects can be sources of vital energy that feed your soul every time you touch or look at them.

This refuge should instill a sense of belonging and security. Make it a space that welcomes you with open, loving arms. Don't be afraid to take up a little room to affirm your place in the world. You are just as deserving of self-care and nurturing as everyone else you love and care for. Build time into your day to visit your space regularly and sit in quiet, even if it's just for a few moments at a time.

Here are some additional suggestions for cultivating a balanced and harmonious life that will heal your body, mind and spirit:

- Take advantage of quiet times of day. Get up just before dawn to sit on the porch or go for a walk and watch the sun rise. Enjoy the landscape before the world awakens.
- Evening's dusk is almost as quiet as the morning's dawn. Welcome the night by gazing at the stars, giving thanks for the blessings of the day.
- If you wake up at night and cannot fall back to sleep, soak in the silence, feel gratitude for it, and focus on taking slow, deep breaths until sleep returns.
- Read or listen to inspirational poetry, calming music, guided meditations, or an uplifting book before falling asleep or beginning your morning. Make your first and last thoughts of the day expansive and full of hope, beauty and love.
- Use the sacred space in your home that you created to simply relax, read a book, listen to calming music, journal or take a nap.
- At night, mask annoying sounds with white noise, such as the nature sounds of running water over rocks or gentle breezes rustling through leaves. Inviting natural, soothing sounds into your living space can be healing and calming.
- Manage noise in your environment by turning off the television, computer, radio and other electronic devices if you are not actively listening or watching something you enjoy. Silence beepers and switch cell phones on vibrate.
- Actively seek out sanctuaries of relative quiet in libraries, museums, art galleries, houses of worship, parks, gardens, walking trails, and meditative spaces. Then visit them regularly.

- Avoid noisy people and places. Cultivate quiet in your life and let silence heal and replenish your mind, body and spirit.
- Commit to having unhurried, quiet time alone. Make silence and solitude a part of your quest for a beautiful and blessed life.

Poet Rainer Maria Rilke wrote, "What is going on in your innermost being is worthy of your whole love."[36] Listening to that voice inside allows you to respond to your physical, emotional and spiritual needs more effectively. You must have a space where you can recharge your energy, heal your wounds, restore your stamina, and gather your courage to continue your life journey. With these periods of restoration, you replenish your creative energy and intuition, fueling creativity and wisdom to give birth to a new vision for your life.

To be calm means being fully awake and present while attending to your inner stirrings. Solitude and silence can be a time of refuge from the busyness of life, allowing you to replenish your energy and stamina. When you withdraw and open yourself to the quiet of your inner being, you become more centered and present to yourself and to others. Solitude does not pull you away from your fellow human beings, but rather helps you become more present and available to foster real relationships.[37]

When you become quiet, your creative energy will flow with abundance to light your path. You may continue to experience adversities that cause feelings of depression, loneliness, anger and confusion, but you will learn to trust that, in the midst of darkness, you are being led to a place of peace and joy.

---

36 Rainer Maria Rilke, *Letters for a Young Poet* (W. W. Norton & Company, 1954), 18–19.

37 Nouwen, *You Are the Beloved*, 46.

Chapter 7
Nurturing Harmony in the Everyday

It can be hard to stay grounded and emotionally steady in the in-between space of endings and beginnings. That's why it's important to develop practices that support your healing and help you regain balance during times of change.

A balanced and harmonious life involves tuning into your inner voice and enjoying an environment that cultivates peace and harmony. There has to be room for energy to flow. Your life force moves through the spaces where you live and work and is of vital importance to your health and happiness. As with your physical, mental and spiritual well-being, when your energy blends with your environment, you feel a deep sense of harmony, comfort and safety. Balancing pleasure and vitality in the places where you habitually spend time is a perfect starting point. Tending to both your internal and external environments is a simple way to energize your life and manifest your goals, hopes and dreams.

Most people are unaware of the effects their senses have on their bodies, minds and spirits. All your senses—sight, sound, smell, touch and taste—have a direct and powerful influence on your nervous system and emotions. What you take in directly affects your thoughts and feelings. Music's endless menu of selections can soothe your soul, energize your spirit, create harmonious intimacy, or invite the urge to dance or sing to your heart's desire. Lavender's scent can relax your nervous system. A funny movie can evoke laughter, triggering the release of endorphins that lifts your mood, creating a joyful spirit.

On the other hand, it's common to become alert and often anxious when you hear sirens, people arguing, screeching tires, and wailing babies. Watching violence on television or in a movie can trigger anxiety, depression and anger, creating disharmony and distress, particularly for individuals who have personally experienced or witnessed traumatic events, such as gun violence, mass shootings, catastrophic weather events, or natural disasters. Just watching news coverage of similar situations can trigger symptoms of anxiety and post-traumatic stress disorder. It is critical to be alert and pay attention to how your external environment affects your internal one.

To create a well-balanced and secure outer world, you might need to lighten up, let go, and allow your circumstances to change, grow and shift in harmony with your inner world. The chaotic energy in a disorderly, cluttered home ripples outward and can create undesirable effects on your health and relationships. Consolidate, organize, discard or donate old or unused items to those who might need or appreciate them.

These activities can have a positive effect on your vitality and boost your creativity. You are able to manifest your health, happiness and well-being when you honor your energy, recognize its crucial connection to your life, and make changes to keep your world balanced and harmonious.

Ask yourself: "Does my environment stimulate living my dreams, visions and purpose? Is the space around me comfortable, nourishing and supportive of my health and happiness?" Creating a harmonious life requires getting in touch with your emotions and instincts, while knowing what you are passionate about ignites the spirit within. Transform the space around you into an environment that invites a deep sense of peace.

Today is all you have—this moment. This concept is at the heart of mindful living. The difference between feeling bored with your circumstances rather than vital and energized lies in elevating your daily life to a richer, more meaningful experience. Much of the enjoyment is in the details—the bigger issues have a way of working themselves out.

When you handle everyday stressors thoughtfully and thoroughly, you may notice how it affects your mood, happiness, vitality and pleasure. Fully lived single days add up to a lifetime lived deeply and well. Small shifts in your daily life have a cumulative effect on your tomorrows.

Breath: The Spirit of Life

THERE IS SPIRIT IN THE AIR we breathe, which is shared by all of creation. It is the medium of exchange between every human and the rest of nature. We breathe in the oxygen that trees and other plants release. We exhale nourishing carbon dioxide. There is no separation between the air we take in and our connection with nature. Breath is the spirit of all life.[38]

You enter and leave this world with one body. It is imperative to learn self-nurturing and healing practices for your emotional, physical, mental and spiritual health. They help you manage the tension within your body, mind and spirit while dealing with the complexities of life. If you've learned these skills, you can endure periods of instability and change with greater ease while also remaining involved in and connected with life.

Breath links your body and mind, as well as your consciousness and unconsciousness. You can manipulate your breathing by simply making the volume louder or softer, varying the length of your inhales and exhales, and adjusting the speed faster or slower. When you intentionally change how you breathe, you influence your autonomic nervous system, which governs involuntary actions.

Fast, loud, short breathing can trigger the sympathetic nervous system, the part of the autonomic nervous system that controls involuntary bodily functions, causing a stress alarm known as the fight-flight-freeze response. This built-in alarm system, also called the stress reaction, is your default setting when your body senses potential danger and has endured throughout the human evolutionary process.

Slow, deep breathing triggers your parasympathetic nervous system, which is a network of nerves that regulates your relaxation response. Feeling calm simply cannot coexist with emotional turmoil. Regardless of the circumstance, intentional, conscious breathing promotes grounding in the present. When

---

38 Douglas-Klotz, *Hidden Gospel*, 59.

you are in the here and now, your thoughts, feelings, needs and desires can be integrated together, which promotes clear communication and restores mental and emotional balance.

Many meditative and contemplative practices begin with calming, conscious breath awareness to tap into the wisdom of the mind/body/spirit connection. Deep breathing increases your oxygen consumption and is a powerful yet easy stress-reduction exercise. Some people unconsciously clench their jaws, teeth or fists in an attempt to contain their emotions. When we say that a particular event has "knocked the wind out of us," we may be subtly holding our breath to avoid feeling "bad." When your breathing is restricted, it is important to tune into your body and identify patterns of emotional and physical tension.

To improve breath awareness, focus on your breathing whenever possible throughout the day. Try making your respirations deeper, slower, quieter and more uniform. Expand your belly outward when inhaling. To deepen breathing, practice exhaling more air at the end of each breath.

When you shift your attention away from emotionally charged thoughts or images, you are able to calm your nervous system. In stressful situations or when you are worried, frustrated or tense, conscious breath awareness allows you to feel relaxed and grounded in the present reality.[39]

By focusing your attention on your breathing, you shut down the incessant inner chatter: the "worry thoughts" about the future and all the "what ifs" about imaginary catastrophes. Likewise, you can also shut down the constant ruminations and "woulda, coulda, shoulda" regrets about things that have already happened. Instead of growing despondent about the past or feeling anxious about the future, both of which you cannot control, breath awareness allows you to focus your attention on the present; namely, what you can control—your body, thoughts and feelings. Conscious breath awareness can have a powerful effect on your physical, emotional and mental health and well-being.[40]

---

39 Pema Chödrön, *Living Beautifully with Uncertainty and Change* (Shambhala Publications Inc., 2012), 45–50.

40 Daniel J. Siegel, *The Mindful Brain: Reflection and Attunement in the Cultivation of Well-Being* (W. W. Norton & Company, 2007), 174–176.

The following two breath exercises can help manage your everyday stressors and improve your mind/body connection.

The first practice is extremely simple and concrete. It can be used whenever fear arises or you find yourself in a stressful situation. When you inhale and really pay attention to your breath, there will be a change in your physical sensations right away. Exhaling, you release the tension in your body and let go of your anxious thoughts. This simple exercise helps you reconnect with reality and allows you to be present to the needs of the moment.

The second exercise is a more meditative practice that allows you to follow your breath from the beginning of its journey to the end, from your inhale to the exhale. This accesses your physical sensations, bringing your mind and body together in the here and now, which strengthens your concentration. With improved awareness of your body and mind, the conditions are ripe for new insights to manifest and for you to transform your suffering into wisdom.

Simple Breath Awareness Practice

This simple breath awareness practice is a quick and easy way to get in touch with your emotions and calm yourself down, to be more centered and present. It can be done anywhere at any time, even when you're driving the car or in a stressful meeting.

As you are learning this practice, you may want to find a quiet place and settle yourself. However, as it becomes more familiar to you, that won't be necessary. Start by allowing your breath to go deep into your diaphragm—drop your shoulders, unclench your teeth, and relax your jaw. Simply notice your breath.

During each full inhalation, slowly count mentally to five as the air enters your lungs. On each exhalation, count again to five as you release the air. Allow each inhale and exhale to be of equal length, and let your belly expand and contract with each full cycle. Breathe deeply and slowly until the intervals between them become relaxed. Try to make your breathing even deeper, slower and more regular.

Notice your heart rate decreasing and your body feeling peaceful. Observe all these sensations for a few minutes without judgment. If at any time you lose focus, simply bring your attention back to the physical sensation of breathing, let go of any thoughts, and return to mentally counting your breaths.

When you are ready, bring your awareness back to your physical body, slowly open your eyes, and return to the present.

If you are paying attention to your breathing, you'll recognize your own unique rhythm and patterns. When you breathe consciously, you encounter all the subtle ways in which you may hold your breath. When you fail to breathe properly, either due to restricted flexibility or flow, it can affect your emotional health or internal psychic condition.[41]

Conscious deep breathing promotes an awareness of your body's sensations and emotions—connecting your physical self to your mind. When you focus your attention on your breathing, you become grounded in reality, allowing your body to relax and your mind to feel calm.

 ## Soulful Self-Reflection: Following the Journey of the Breath

Many breathing practices focus on following the sensation of your breath's journey throughout your body. This meditative practice, adapted from Neil Douglas-Klotz,[42] draws your conscious attention to the ebb and flow of your breathing as you seek a deeper connection to your unique rhythm. This awareness provides you with insight into your emotional health, allowing you to monitor and manage your stress more effectively.

> Find a quiet place and settle yourself. Begin by lying down or sitting comfortably for a few minutes. Close your eyes and place one hand lightly over your heart. Rest the other gently on your belly. Allow your breath to go deep into your diaphragm, drop your

---

41 Douglas-Klotz, *Hidden Gospel*, 46, 48–49.

42 Douglas-Klotz, *Hidden Gospel*, 47–48.

shoulders, unclench your teeth, and relax your jaw. Simply notice your breathing until the intervals between become slow and relaxed.

There are many distinct moments to pay attention to in the breath's journey—the experience is much like the ebb and flow of an ocean wave. There is the sensation as the breath enters your lungs, a moment of fullness when you pause, and then the tidal pull out toward emptiness.

At each twist and turn, your body responds in a particular way. You may notice a presence or an absence of sensation, thought or emotion, either at the beginning, middle or end. Or you may feel you want to stay longer in one part of the journey.

Slow your breathing until you can sense the inner workings of your body. Feel the gentle rise and fall of your belly, breathing in vital energy, and how it calms your whole being. Allow the rhythm of your breathing and your heartbeat to harmonize. Simply notice all the sensations without judgment for several minutes.

After you find and maintain a calm internal rhythm, slowly open your eyes and bring your awareness back to the present. Can you sense how that deep calmness permeates everything? Try to maintain this state of serenity and self-compassion as you return to the busyness of your life.

If you do this exercise daily over several weeks, you may begin to see a correlation between the quality of your breathing and events that provoke an emotional response.

Breath awareness can become a barometer for the emotional weather in your life. The flexibility of the energy flowing through your body not only indicates your internal emotional health, but also how connected you are to others and the world around you.

With practice, the resting state of your mind and body will become more peaceful, and you will experience more resilience in your daily life. Breath awareness and good breathing habits enhance your mental, emotional and physical well-being, whether you practice them alone or in combination with other stress management practices.

Chapter 8
Practicing Inner Knowing Through Contemplation

Meditative and contemplative practices allow you to experience your inner knowing. A simplistic version to describe this might be: something that seems like a deeper feeling or intuition. When we begin to connect with and know who we are and what we truly believe, it leaves us with our own indelible truth. This inner knowing can guide us through the transitions in life to bring us to a place of peace and contentment.

In the book *Yes, And... Daily Meditations*, bestselling author Richard Rohr wrote that "the central things in life, although spiritually perceptible, remain invisible, and can be easily overlooked by our inattention and busy lives."[43] Rather than knowledge gained through facts or reason, inner knowing is described as "intuitive cognition," a more integrated awareness than mere reason alone. Rohr notes that it becomes "more a process than a conclusion, more an experience than a dogma, more a personal relationship than an idea." With inner knowledge, you no longer need to justify your beliefs. You have found your inner truth and the confidence that comes with that, so you no longer need to be afraid to speak your true values, beliefs, ideas or opinions. Meditation and contemplative practices allow you to focus on the center of

---

43 Richard Rohr, *Yes, And... Daily Meditations* (Franciscan Media, 2013), 6.

your being, where you'll discover a world of beauty and depth that reflects your wisdom. Being faithful to your truth leads to a growing awareness of the awe and wonder of life.

To be human is to search for purpose and meaning. His Holiness the Dalai Lama teaches that "the purpose of our existence is to seek happiness." For some, this may seem like common sense. But life is not easy. We all have our struggles, and maintaining a state of happiness may seem next to impossible as a result.

Western psychiatrist Howard C. Cutler, MD, engaged the Dalai Lama in a series of conversations published in 1998 as *The Art of Happiness*. In it, the Dalai Lama advises that happiness is "determined more by the state of one's mind than by one's external conditions, circumstances or events" and that it can be achieved through the conscious training of the mind.[44] He says, "In terms of our enjoying a happy day-to-day existence, the greater the level of calmness of the mind, the greater our peace of mind, the greater our ability to enjoy a happy and joyful life."[45]

In the Buddhist tradition, "liberation from suffering" describes the calm awareness of mind/body consciousness. Our pathway to happiness and well-being depends on what is happening in the interrelationship of the mind, body and spirit. Recent neurological studies have demonstrated that what we think and feel, and how we react to things, shapes our brain. Mental activity, whether conscious or unconscious, can reform the brain's neural structure in a variety of ways. In 1949, Donald Hebb was the first neuroscientist to posit that "neurons that fire together wire together."[46] Simply stated, whatever we think about redirects the neuropathways of our brain.

Meditation is a powerful way to restructure the mind and is key to reducing stress and optimizing emotional happiness and well-being. It has its origins in practices that are over 7,000 years old, but it has only been since the 1960s that it's become more mainstream in Western medicine and culture. It is a simple

---

44 H H Dalai Lama and Howard C. Cutler, *The Art of Happiness: A Handbook for Living* (Riverhead Books, 1998), 16, 20.

45 Dalai Lama and Cutler, *Art of Happiness* 25–26.

46 Donald O. Hebb, *The Organization of Behavior* (John Wiley & Sons, 1949).

strategy that brings mindful attention to our thoughts, feelings and physical sensations—the good, the bad, the neutral—without judgment. The emphasis is always on *what* is happening, not *why* it is happening.

Jon Kabat-Zinn, a pioneer in mind/body medicine, founded the Mindfulness-Based Stress Reduction (MBSR) program at the University of Massachusetts Medical Center in 1979, and his MBSR method has been shown to have a positive effect on physical and mental health.[47] Mindfulness meditation has been implemented in both medical and mental health venues for reducing stress and managing anxiety, depression and chronic pain, as well as decreasing symptoms of autoimmune illnesses, such as rheumatoid arthritis, blood pressure, cortisol levels, asthma, type 2 diabetes, and cancer.

Mindfulness is the awareness that emerges through paying attention, purposefully and nonjudgmentally, to the moment to moment unfolding of life's experiences. When you practice it, you can activate your body's natural calming response to a stressful event simply by paying attention to what is happening in your mind and body. Mindfulness requires a commitment and a willingness to be present with whatever emerges. It is about being fully awake in your life. Learning to trust what may feel overwhelming has the potential to create and sustain emotional balance and transform your inner power and wisdom.

The art of all meditative practices is bringing attention to the moment. Mindfulness depends on cultivating three basic skills:

1. noticing and naming your emotions and thoughts as they arise;
2. befriending sensations in your body;
3. consciously letting go of your thoughts and reclaiming the full range of your emotional sensitivity.

Relinquishing your thoughts, desires and judgments through mindfulness means simply releasing the ideas your mind gets in the habit of fixating on, including those of yesterday and tomorrow. You do not have to go on a journey with every thought that comes to mind or that you struggle to make sense of. If nothing grabs onto them as they arise, they move on.

---

47 Jon Kabat-Zinn, *Full Catastrophic Living: Using the Wisdom of Your Body and Mind to Face Stress, Pain, and Illness* (Bantam Books, 2013).

Think of it like being a mirror—your mind notices something in front of it, registers what it is without holding on to it, and lets it go. You do not have to cling to the random thoughts that pull you away from fully experiencing the present.

Mindfulness offers a way of waking up from a life on autopilot and being sensitive to the novelty in your everyday experiences. It is about perceiving the exquisite vividness of each moment.

When you cultivate the meditative practice of sitting in silence and intentionally turning inward, you will experience calmness and awareness in your body and mind, and your soul will be filled with awe and wonder in life's ordinary moments.

The following two mindfulness practices teach you how to be fully awake and present in your life. The essence of the first practice is to just sit and give your full attention to your mind and your body, while the second practice is a longer mindfulness meditation that helps to clear your mind of intrusive thoughts without judgment.

There are many ways to meditate, and the best practice of all is the one you will do. You can meditate while standing, walking or lying down, but most people do it while sitting on a chair or cushion. Start with shorter periods of time, even just five minutes. Longer sessions will usually help you go deeper, but they take some practice.

Just Sitting Meditation

The simplest form of mindfulness meditation in the Zen tradition is called *shikantaza* (she-khan-tah-zah), a Japanese phrase that loosely translates to "just sitting." It is nothing other than sitting quietly, in silence and solitude, so the restless mind can be keenly felt.

This is a basic meditation technique to train your mind to be still, to let go of unwanted head chatter, and to focus your full attention on being present in your body. With practice, your concentration will improve.

When you need to think deeply about a task or a problem, use this meditation to sit quietly and gain clarity and resolution with greater ease.

Before you start, decide how long to meditate and set a timer. Find a comfortable, quiet place to sit, where you can focus and not be disturbed. Begin by paying attention to your breathing. Keep yourself still, listen to your mind, feel your body, and remain calm. Allow your thoughts and feelings to move through your consciousness without resistance, not putting walls around seemingly negative events and emotions, but granting them space and acceptance. Every experience is worthy of your attention. When your mind fills the silence with conversation or your attention strays, that is normal and expected. Notice it has wandered and gently refocus on the present moment with your breath. Be curious. See what happens when you attempt to "just sit."

Mindfulness Meditation

Mindfulness meditation uses your breath to bring your attention back to the present. Life is unpredictable. There will always be unexpected events or potential challenges. Learning to be calm in the here and now allows you to be fully engaged in your life and provides an invaluable tool for coping when difficulties arise. This powerful mindfulness technique teaches you how to live wholeheartedly every day.

Here is a basic mindfulness meditation practice for you to follow.

Before you start, decide how long to meditate and set a timer. Find a quiet place where you will be undisturbed. Sit on a cushion with your legs crossed or on a chair with your feet flat on the floor. Adopt a comfortable posture with your back straight but not stiff, hands folded gently in your lap. Slowly lower your gaze. Simply sit, not doing anything and not focused on anything other than your body and mind.

To begin this meditation, take a long, deep breath and relax. Allow yourself to be led to the silence within. Bring your awareness to the sensations of your breathing. Don't try to control it; let it be whatever it is. Sense the cool air coming in and warm air going out. Allow your breath to go deep into your diaphragm—drop your shoulders, unclench your teeth, and relax your jaw. Notice each breath from beginning to end. You may want to count them softly to ten and then begin again.

It's normal for your mind to wander. When it does, simply bring your focus back to your breathing, using it as a kind of anchor. See if you can stay attentive for ten breaths in a row.

Be aware of whatever else is moving through your mind. Notice any thoughts and feelings, wishes and plans, images and memories—all coming and going. Let them be what they are without getting caught up in them. When your mind wanders, gently recognize it and, without judgment, bring your attention back to your breathing. Be gentle and kind to yourself. You are not trying to make your mind blank. Simply accept the distraction, smile and think *Thank you for sharing*. Then, let it pass through your awareness.

Notice the changing nature of what passes through your mind. Observe how it feels to get caught up in your thoughts, and how it feels to let them go by.

Become increasingly absorbed in your breath, letting go of everything else. Be open to the simple pleasure of breathing. Be aware of the growing sense of peacefulness. With practice, you will be able to stay present for longer periods of time.

When you are ready, bring the meditation to an end. Slowly open your eyes and bring your awareness back to your external environment. Notice how you feel without stress or strain in your body. Gently open yourself to calm relaxation and an increased sense of yourself.

Meditative practices can take many forms: sitting in solitude and silence, mindfulness meditation, calming breath awareness, prayer, spiritual reading, journaling, yoga, tai chi, walking meditation, reading poetry, making art, and gardening, to name a few. You may use just one of these methods or a constellation of them. New practices may emerge as your life changes, or your favorites may be present for years but vary over time. The key to reaping the rewards of meditation is to develop a routine practice, no matter how brief.

Studies have shown that regular meditation promotes mindfulness. It is to the mind what aerobic exercise is to the body. The main objective is to make it less about the externals and more about focusing on your inner awakening and letting go. Meditation is the foundation of changing your brain and thus changing your life for the better.

A Contemplative Path to Inner Knowing

A CONTEMPLATIVE WAY OF LIFE means observing your life carefully, paying close attention to what is happening, and recognizing moments where you awaken to its beauty and abundance. In the midst of your busyness, you might never notice the ordinary things all around. Then, out of the blue, something will catch your eye, and you will pause for a moment in awe and reflect on what awakened you. Notice a brilliant sunset, a child's laugh, the vibrant iridescent ruby-throated hummingbird at the backyard feeder—and you nearly quit breathing. In an ordinary moment, you are absorbed by the breathtaking beauty experienced in an extraordinary moment of awakening.

These contemplative experiences circle through the everyday occurrences in our lives, whether we see them in nature, our relationships, or times of difficulty. Life flows in a cyclical pattern. Awe provokes awakening, which in turn elicits awe. You may be overcome with joy when you hold your child's hand or witness the birth of your grandchild. Or you may be overwhelmed with heartache as you lie curled beside your dying spouse the moment he takes his final breath. The veil is pulled back, and life seems inexhaustibly holy and mysterious. Your existence has been shaped by losses, enriched by blessings, and expanded by nature's beauty. Encounters with the sacred embolden us to cultivate stillness and simple awareness.

Contemplative practices have existed within the Christian tradition for almost two millennia. These methods teach an embodied experience of unity *with* spirit rather than a merely cognitive knowledge *about* spirit.[48]

As we learned from Richard Rohr earlier, it takes patience and practice to reach a sense of inner knowing, which grants us a new understanding of the world in times of great uncertainty. There are no quick or easy answers. You must proceed by waiting and practicing attentiveness, which often involves remaining open to new insights.[49] This contemplative way of living holds the tension of the unknown and invites "waiting patiently for the gaps to be filled in."

---

48 Richard Rohr and Patrick Boland, *Every Thing Is Sacred* (Convergent Books, 2021), 31.

49 Richard Rohr, *The Universal Christ: How A Forgotten Reality Can Change Everything We See, Hope For, And Believe* (Convergent Books, 2021), 8.

Contemplation never rushes to judgment or easy answers. Instead, it relies on a loving search for inner truth rather than the need to be in control.

Living a contemplative life invites you to hold the uneasiness caused by the unknown and mysterious. The uncertainties of tomorrow and the complexities of our relationships, hurts and hopes all invite us beyond mere cognitive thought to seek inner knowing. Contemplation allows us to look at the world with a humble attitude of acceptance of things we may never fully understand. There will always be more to learn, more to see, and more ways to experience extraordinary moments of awakening. Rather than growing despondent with life's uncertainties, contemplation helps us appreciate the present.

Soulful Self-Reflection: Practicing the Lectio Divina

In the monastic tradition, the contemplative practice of lingering and exploring the depths of a text is called *Lectio Divina*. It is a way of going deeper than comprehending words, using them to give answers, or solving immediate problems. *Lectio Divina* asks: How can we use sacred texts, poetry, soulful writings, and life experiences to discover spiritual truths, inner awareness, and new visions for our life?

Take a few moments to read the following text in a contemplative way. Focus your awareness on your thoughts, emotions and physical sensations, then write what this reflection evokes in you.

> Find a quiet place and settle yourself. Begin by sitting and breathing gently, inhaling long and deep and then exhaling in a slow and relaxed manner. Allow yourself to be led to the silence within.
>
> Select an uplifting text or experience you'd like to reflect on, or use the following verses from Proverbs 4:11-13.
>
>> I instruct you in the way of wisdom
>> and lead you along straight paths.
>> When you walk, your steps will not be hampered;
>> when you run, you will not stumble.

> Hold on to instruction, do not let it go;
> guard it well, for it is your life.

Whichever you choose, slowly read the words or think about the experience.

Using the Proverbs excerpt as an example, use these strategies to contemplate its meaning:

- Read this passage in a contemplative way. Instead of analyzing each line, pay attention to the words, phrases and images that speak most to you, even if you do not fully understand them in the moment.
- When you do your second and third readings, pause between each one. Consider whether there is a particular word or phrase that stands out to you.
- Journal about whatever comes to mind. (For example, any memories you recall, emotions you feel, or thoughts you have.) How is this passage related to your life right now?
- Read the passage one last time. Allow yourself a few moments of silence before returning to your day.

Meditative and contemplative practices go beyond your unconscious mind and allow your inner knowing to change you from the inside out. When you regularly devote time to meditation or contemplative practices, you enter into the depths of your soul without judgment or comparison with others. Over time, as clarity of thought begins to emerge, you cultivate nonjudgmental openness within yourself and for whatever arises within your consciousness. You claim the unconditional love that was given to you at your birth.

When you practice meditation or contemplation, your awareness of your spiritual self takes on new meaning, becoming part of who you truly are. Without self-knowledge and inner knowing, you cannot experience the miracle of grace and forgiveness. Slowly, with consistent practice, you become aware of the wondrous surprises occurring every moment in the natural world.

Poetry as a Sacred Practice

READING AND WRITING HAVE OFTEN been associated with healing our wounds, finding peace and harmony in our soul, and reclaiming and revitalizing our mind, body and spirit. In ancient Egypt, libraries were known as *psyches iatreion*, a healing place of the soul. During the Renaissance, poetry was thought to reduce distress and to be soothing. At the beginning of the nineteenth century, the American psychiatric community advocated reading and writing as therapeutic techniques.

Poetry and prose have a humanizing influence that can carry us to heights of spiritual insight and realizations. They are the great metronome for all humanity, generating empathy for others and allowing us to feel our relationships more deeply. The writing we read connects us all—different worlds, different ideas, different people, and different experiences. When we feel a kinship with others, it is much more difficult to oppress them.

Paying attention to the stirrings of spirit while reading poetry allows us to explore our inner terrain, soothes our soul, and encourages the contemplation of our truth. Poetry poses profound questions and leads us to revelations of the soul. Its rhythm and magic open a door for us to go deeper into our own experiences, joys and sorrows, and unravel the nuances and subtleties of our feelings and life experiences. Robert Frost said, "A poem begins with a lump in the throat."[50]

A great poem is a temple, a place to feel and vanish into the sacred world within. We are compelled to ask, "If a poem does not evoke deep emotion, is it a great poem?"

Poets are experts in the art of metaphor. The word *metaphor* comes from the Greek word to "carry across." A great poem carries us across the dissimilarities between us into commonality, evoking within us the epiphany that there is only one world, and all is sacred within it. Reading poetry contemplatively can be a sacred practice. By meditating on the words, we dig deep into the underground river that flows within each of us—our shared common waters with all humanity.

Poetry is not only life-sustaining, but can have a profound, if not perceptible, way of changing the course of a life. A great poem tells the truth.

---

50 Robert Frost, "Some Definitions" in *Collected Poems, Prose, and Plays* (Library of America, 1995), 701.

It calls us to pay attention to the world around us and opens us to the universe within. And it has a way of rescuing humanity from oblivion.

I discovered the healing power of poetry when I first read David Whyte's "Sweet Darkness" from *The House of Belonging* during a difficult time in my life.

> You must learn one thing.
> The world was made to be free in.
>
> Give up all the other worlds
> except the one to which you belong.
>
> Sometimes it takes darkness and the sweet
> confinement of your aloneness
> to learn
>
> anything or anyone
> that does not bring you alive
>
> is too small for you.[51]

I felt the final lines speak directly to me. "Sometimes it takes darkness and the sweet confinement of your aloneness to learn anything or anyone that does not bring you alive is too small for you." That poem showed up at exactly the right moment to begin a conversation that had been lurking below the surface: *How had my life become too small?*

I began exploring poems—not just reading them, but developing rich relationships with the ones that not only infused me with their wisdom, but actually brought energy and vibrancy to my body and soul. I became fascinated with the healing power of poetry and its ability to unlock the richness of our inner life. When we pay attention, something in us wakes up and moves us closer to who we're meant to be.

For centuries, we have chanted, sung and written poems to remind ourselves of what it means to be human. Poetry communicates the heart and soul of a populace in a way prose cannot. It has been a catalyst for inspiring innovative thinking and engaging discussions about life's most perplexing questions. It has been used to facilitate connections, inspire imaginative thought, and evoke

---

51 David Whyte, "Sweet Darkness" in *The House of Belonging* (Many Rivers Press,1997), 23.

courageous conversations. The power of poetry represents the sanctity of what we hold most dear, whether that be hope, love, equality or compassion.

A poem is more than words on a page. It is breath, sound and rhythm. Like a shaman's drum or a Sanskrit chant, a poem vibrates with the rhythm of our heartbeat. Most of them offer their full magic only when wedded with a human voice. Reading poetry aloud has a physical effect on your body. The phrasing changes your breathing patterns, and the sounds resonate within the structures of your bones and muscles. Scientific research shows your brainwaves, breathing patterns, and pulse rate change while reciting a poem. Its physical elements literally create the biochemical circumstances for healing and insight.[52] A good poem has the power to calm your soul and open your mind to levels beyond ordinary thinking.

I invite you to explore the healing power of poetry. Find an inspiring poem that resonates with you and befriend it. Read the verses aloud. It is important to give voice to poetry, even if no one is listening. If you read too quickly, you may not "get" it. A poem needs time, quiet, solitude and space to work its magic.

Once you find stanzas you love, write your favorite lines on cards as a motivational tool. Read one upon awakening or before retiring, or use them as inspiration when facing a demanding situation in your life. Verses that bring harmony and clarity are available anytime you may need calm reassurance.

Journaling: A Healing and Creative Expression

WRITING FACILITATES THE CREATIVE EXPRESSION of our inner stirrings, which can lead to powerful revelations and healing grace. Enlightened practitioners, including Swiss psychiatrist Carl Jung, used private journaling to treat specific mental disorders. The simple act of putting words on paper and telling your own stories often brings relief, like having an enormous weight lifted from your shoulders. When you listen to your inner voice, you gain a deep security from knowing your inner truth.

---

52 Kim Rosen, "The Medicine of Poetry: How Words Can Save Your Life" in *Spirituality and Health*, July–August 2012, 57.

In her revolutionary book *Writing Down the Bones*, Natalie Goldberg compared writing to a Zen meditation that helps penetrate the unconscious mind. Goldberg described her practice as "first thoughts." The aim is to:

> burn through to first thoughts, to the place where energy is unobstructed by politeness or the internal censor, to the place where you are writing what your mind actually sees and feels, not what it *thinks* it should see or feel.[53]

Goldberg recommends handwriting over using a keyboard to connect the movement of the body with the rhythm of the soul.

Poet and author Julia Cameron outlines a similar practice she refers to as "morning pages" as a way to find "our spiritual bearings." In her book *The Artist's Way*, she advocates writing three pages in a continuous stream-of-consciousness upon awakening. By writing in longhand, our unedited thoughts and feelings are "loose, messy, disorganized, disjointed and flighty."[54] Cameron believes that by writing these morning pages, we connect with the "voice of our soul" to reveal our unspoken wishes and dreams.

Journal writing is a self-nurturing practice that connects the healing power of our psychological world with our spiritual world. G. Lynn Nelson describes it as "the interplay between language and psyche" in her book *Writing and Being*.[55] Journaling is not a diary or a daily log of events or things in your life. Nor is it writing a research paper. Nelson describes it as a "me-search" into the unexplored territory of mystery and wonder deep within one's own soul that will "almost invariably lead to a kind of lifting and lightening and opening up." She goes on to say that journal writing is like "entering the river" and allowing it to flow wherever it takes you.

Journaling provides a private, safe place to let go of formal constraints and rules of grammar, spelling and punctuation. It's a place to be creative and feel free to let down your protective shield and be your true self. The process

---

53 Natalie Goldberg, *Writing Down the Bones: Freeing the Writer Within* (Shambhala, 1986).

54 Julia Cameron, *The Artist's Way: Spiritual Path to Higher Creativity* (Tarcher Putnam, 1992).

55 G. Lynn Nelson, *Writing and Being: Embracing Your Life Through Creative Journaling* (New World Press, 2004).

is a spontaneous flow of words from within. Some pages may be written as a stream-of-consciousness, while others are a hodgepodge of notes, observations, feelings and even drawings. As you continue the practice, you will develop your own unique style. You may notice you write and feel things that seem to emerge from deep within—gifts from your soul that lead you closer to your truest self.

Your journal can be anything from loose sheets of paper in a folder to an expensive, leather-bound book. The only criteria are that it is something you feel comfortable writing in and that it invites the flow of your words. Create a sacred space for journaling that is welcoming and peaceful, where you can tell your stories, heal your wounds, and find peace within your heart. Writing connects you to the mystery and power of your inner voice.

Soulful Self-Reflection: Healing through Journaling

We have this one life. We live it day by day. Some days pass quickly. Others, more slowly. In those calmer moments, something might catch your attention, making you curious to know more. Journaling is an opportunity to slow down, be still, and go deeper. Writing is a way to tap into your inner voice.

A writing practice is a perfect complement to a meditation practice. It is the art of being present with your life and with your pen. It promotes having a relationship with your mind, accepting your thoughts, whatever they are, and getting to know yourself on a deeper level. Writing is a creative tool that can bring a sense of empowerment and healing grace.

Here are two journaling exercises that invite you to put your life on the line, so to speak, and to journey inward with an inquisitive spirit.

The first exercise is to write about a memorable experience that continues to fill your heart with delight and purpose. In the second exercise, journaling becomes an instrument of healing. While bad things happen as well as wonderful things, writing can play a powerful role in transforming adversity into growth and meaning.

These two journaling exercises capture very different periods and aspects of your life, although they both focus on cultivating deep listening. I encourage you to experience each of these practices, but not in the same sitting. Pick one that resonates with you now and leave the other for another time. Learn to trust that still, small voice within, which is your intuition. Everyone has this capability.

You only need time and intention to develop it. Let yourself take this inner journey and see what unfolds.

Memories That Bring Joy and Happiness

Everything that's ever happened to you throughout your life is stored in your memory bank, just beneath the surface of awareness. Something you see or hear or feel may trigger a recollection, or an image will come to mind, and you're whisked back in time as if that moment is happening right now. It may not be a sensational moment, like winning the lottery, but perhaps a quiet instant when your whole awareness shifted and you gained new insight about your life and yourself. Or, it may be an incident or situation that became a turning point, one that led you in a different direction or created a vision you never imagined.

When you reflect on and journal about meaningful experiences in your life, you may gain insights into how you have been sustained by these memorable people, places and events. What joy and happiness these recollections bring when you claim the wisdom revealed!

We all have memories that sustain us and offer gifts of intrinsic value that are priceless. These may include:
- memories of home and family roots
- recollections of powerful lessons learned
- remembered acts of love or compassion
- epiphanies just waiting to be claimed

Write about a time in your life that brought joy and happiness. It can be a significant life-changing moment or an ordinary memory that continues to bring sustaining wisdom and pleasure.

Find a quiet place and settle yourself. Begin by sitting and breathing gently. Select a special memory from your past that you cherish. Write freely about the people, places and events that provide you with gifts of self-worth, joy and happiness. Let your thoughts, feelings and insights flow without explanation or concern about proper grammar or spelling. Listen to your inner voice. Go slowly and respect the process.

When your recollection is complete, sit with it for a few moments. Now ask yourself these questions:

1. What made me think of this particular memory?
2. Does it reveal any significant patterns that relate to my life today?
3. If so, write about this connection and see where it leads you.

Give thanks for the people who have nurtured and supported you on this journey. Be grateful for all the events that are woven into the uniquely beautiful tapestry that is your life story.

Writing Can Heal Your Soul

Transitions provide opportunities to reexamine your desires, dreams and goals, and explore new possibilities and exciting adventures. When you refuse to acknowledge that impermanence is an inevitable part of life's ever-changing landscape, you suffer greatly. Reluctance to face change—in yourself, your life, your relationships, and the world—can become a veil of denial that prevents you from moving toward a brighter vision of the future.

The power of journal writing comes from releasing the truth that resides deep within you. In this exercise, you will explore an aspect of your life that needs healing or something about yourself that needs to be changed so you can experience the promise of a new beginning.

Find a quiet place and settle yourself. Begin by sitting and breathing gently. To gain a new perspective, it may be necessary to heal what has gone before. Reflect on an old, destructive pattern (for example, pleasing or enabling others) that may have helped you survive a period in your life, but no longer serves you. Let go of worn-out beliefs or traits (such as perfectionism or procrastination) that keep you stuck, unable to fulfill your full potential, or prevent you from living life wholeheartedly.

After a few minutes, answer these questions:

- Where do I feel trapped or mired in my life? What am I really tired of?
- What parts of myself have I neglected, ignored or suppressed?
- Am I clinging to security when change is called for?
- What changes are happening in my life that require my attention?

Select one of the questions above or pose one of your own to explore and write about. Let your thoughts, feelings and insights flow without explanation or concern about proper grammar or spelling. Listen to your inner voice. Go slowly and respect the process.

Using the insights you've gained from this exercise, craft a plan for the changes you want to make in your life.

An inescapable condition of living is that we will all experience the wonderful and the terrible reality of life's endings and beginnings. Developing journaling as a practice for gaining insight and wisdom allows the expression of your inner voice and deepest truths. Writing provides a healing and creative process for uncovering the mystery of your life's journey.

Chapter 9
Accepting Change, Trusting the Soul

When I had a near-death experience, my life was changed forever. For ten years, I experienced periodic episodes of intense, jolting pain in the right side of my face, like having an electric shock, that stopped me in my tracks until it subsided. These episodes would persist for a month or so and then go away, only to return with a vengeance.

I had just completed my clinical psychology internship at Southwestern Medical Center in Dallas when the right-side facial pain returned and took up residence, disrupting my postdoctoral supervision year and my preparation for the national psychological licensing exam. Suspecting an oral problem, I made an appointment with my dentist, who diagnosed trigeminal neuralgia, a chronic pain condition.

Trigeminal neuralgia, also known as tic douloureux, is a disorder of the fifth cranial nerve located close to the brainstem. The condition is caused by a blood vessel pressing against the trigeminal nerve, known as vascular compression. Over time, the pulse of the artery rubbing against the nerve wears away the myelin lining, leaving it exposed and extremely sensitive. According to medical reports, trigeminal neuralgia is the most excruciating pain known to humanity.

Over the next two months, my pain manifested daily as sudden, excruciating, shock-like episodes in my right jaw and cheek. These experiences lasted anywhere from a few seconds to minutes and were triggered by gentle touching, speaking, chewing or even the slightest movement or sensation on my face. The agony became unrelenting and debilitating to the point of being unable to talk, eat or drink. A gentle breeze would trigger a spasm lasting several minutes. My sole mode of communication was writing, and I only ingested liquids by sucking them through a straw on the opposite side of my mouth.

After two months of unsuccessfully trying different antiseizure medications, neurosurgery became the only option to alleviate the spasms. At that point, its intensity had become so debilitating and unbearable that, for the first time in my life, I contemplated suicide to escape the unrelenting pain.

My primary care physician made a referral to one of the few neurosurgeons in my state experienced in performing trigeminal nerve surgery. The doctor confirmed my diagnosis, and the procedure was scheduled for the following week.

The six-hour neurosurgery revealed the trigeminal nerve had attached to a blood vessel at the brainstem. Detaching the nerve from the vessel resulted in permanent damage to my trigeminal nerve and complete loss of feeling on the whole right side of my face.

During my recovery in the ICU, I experienced an allergic reaction to medications and brain swelling, causing my heart and breathing functions to shut down and triggering a "code blue" emergency. I recall hearing a nurse ask, "What will we tell her family in the morning if she doesn't make it?"

The next thing I remember is a near-death experience where I was given the choice to return to my current life or surrender to death. I chose to go on living, knowing my purpose was unfulfilled. My two children were young adults just starting their own independent lives, careers and relationships, which I wanted to be a part of and witness. Furthermore, having recently completed my doctoral internship and being in the midst of preparing for my licensing exam, I was at a crucial point where new professional opportunities were unfolding. My near-death experience had a profound impact on my commitment to live each day with purpose and meaning.

Grateful to be alive and pain-free, I experienced visual hallucinations during my first night in a private room due to the interactions of pain and steroid medications. I informed the nurse about them and asked to have the lights turned on to provide relief from this very unusual psychiatric episode. I spent the night enjoying the image of a toy Christmas train circling round and round my hospital room with me riding atop the engine. Knowing the cause of the hallucinations allowed me to remain calm and to be amused amid a profoundly serious and challenging medical crisis. Whenever I recall that night, I still chuckle at my Christmas train ride while giving thanks to my extraordinary medical team and the hospital care that brought relief to my pain and saved my life.

During my recovery at home, I experienced many side effects, including severe vertigo, double vision, dizziness, nausea, vomiting, motor imbalance, auditory difficulties, tinnitus and periodic slowing of my involuntary breathing—all complications of surgical swelling at the brainstem. It took several months before I could return to my normal daily activities, manage household chores, and drive a vehicle. Having lost all the feeling in the right side of my face, I had to relearn how to move my mouth, tongue, lips and face to talk, eat and smile normally and effectively.

My recovery taught me patience, compassion and self-care. One of my greatest fears was that I might have suffered brain damage and all my years of doctoral education and training would be lost because I would be unable to complete my postdoctoral supervision and pass the written and oral psychological licensing exams. Likewise, I was concerned that, without facial movement, I would be viewed as distant and uncaring.

Rather than allowing my fears and anxiety to hamper my efforts to adapt to these new physical changes, I used my spiritual courage and strength, gained through previous challenges, to keep moving forward. Eventually, I regained full physical and emotional functioning despite my facial numbness. With patience and perseverance, I accomplished my professional goals, passing the national and state licensing exams and opening my psychology practice the following year.

Through my health crisis, I gained the gifts of patience, resilience and self-compassion that have been a source of strength and gratitude throughout my life. My pre- and post-operative experiences gave me an understanding of what other individuals with debilitating severe physical and mental disorders and illnesses endure. I gained firsthand knowledge of how intense, excruciating, chronic pain can lead to suicidal ideation and what it is like to have visual hallucinations. These invaluable experiences taught me empathy, compassion, resilience and courage, and have brought me a deeper sense of purpose, a greater appreciation for my relationships, and gratitude for the miracle of health and the gift of life.

For years following my neurosurgery, I didn't tell anyone about my near-death experience out of fear of not being believed or people thinking I was crazy. After reading several books and listening to others tell their personal stories, I became more comfortable selectively sharing my experience. My brush with near-death taught me about the fragility of life and to recognize that any moment, without warning, it can be over in a heartbeat.

Today, my greatest fear is not death, but rather, not living life to the fullest while I am alive. As I reflect on that pivotal moment, I am grateful for what that near-death experience taught me about who I am and what my purpose is.

Threads of Continuity

BY HONORING THE SACREDNESS OF life's continually evolving process, you recognize the interconnectedness of endings and beginnings. In this betwixt and between space, embracing change requires time, patience and an abundance of courage and stamina. You must grieve your losses, evaluate your relationships, adjust attachments in your external world, and renegotiate your current needs. You may feel compelled to defend who you are, and it may seem daunting to consider doing anything to disturb the life you have built. In this in-between space, you may experience a shift in awareness that ignites unconscious memories of past transitions, triggering chaotic and disordered thoughts and feelings that seem to make no sense or have no reason to come up in the present. It is only later that you recognize that what is happening now is similar to a past transition.

In her insightful book *Willing to Learn*, Mary Catherine Bateson writes:

> Much of the coping with discontinuity has to do with discovering threads of continuity. You cannot adjust to change unless you can recognize some analogy between your old situation and your new situation. Without that analogy, you cannot transfer learning. You cannot apply skills. If you can recognize a problem that you've solved before, in however different a guise, you have a much greater chance of solving that problem in the new situation. That recognition is critical to the transfer of learning.[56]

---

[56] Mary Catherine Bateson, *Willing to Learn: Passages of Personal Discovery* (Steerforth Press, 2004), 70.

Transitions are smoother when you reach for skills and practices that were refined previously—how you confronted problem-solving, made adaptations, and developed coping skills—and then transfer that wisdom to your current situation. By using these threads, you dispel the instability and confusion while remaining grounded during the treachery of transition. When you draw on the wisdom and knowledge gained from past changes in your life, you can craft a new vision for your future.

Letting go of the old and embracing the new allows you to transfer your wisdom to fresh problems and current choices, weaving together old interests and connections while welcoming novel activities and new relationships. Beginnings become invitations to explore unfamiliar places, meet people, and take advantage of unique opportunities for self-discovery while remaining grounded in familiar territory. By weaving together threads of continuity, you make your journey smoother and move forward into a brighter vision for tomorrow.

When you pause in the midst of change to honor all you've already endured, you uncover the courage and confidence to release your fears and face upheaval with an openness to new opportunities and possibilities.

As your perspective on life's struggles shifts, you grow in compassion—for yourself and for others—and recognize that every transition invites you to live differently. By embracing how painful endings shape what comes next, the broken pieces of your life come together, transforming you into a wiser, more resilient, compassionate and authentic version of yourself.

Every experience offers lessons and a chance to discover your inner truth. The life-altering, turbulent transition of my divorce changed my trajectory and led me to a vocation that has brought purpose and meaning to my life. Later, after my neurosurgery, the transformational question that inspired and encouraged me was, "What are the values and beliefs that provide a constant source of strength and courage for me during this health crisis?"

Since I recognized the interrelatedness of my old and new challenges, I could apply the coping skills and wisdom I'd gained previously. With the support and encouragement of family and friends, I gained a sense of stability and comfort during a time of instability and recovery. Slowly, with patience and perseverance, I completed my goal of becoming a licensed psychologist and followed my calling to help others who are suffering. Although every new transition I encounter remains challenging, I have learned that, by never letting go of my threads of continuity and trusting my wise heart, a new vision will unfold that aligns with my true self and purpose.

Successfully navigating life's adversities yields many lessons. Your struggles will become your greatest teachers when you search for wisdom and self-knowledge. Doing so enables you to discover threads of continuity that become skills and practices that in turn help you adapt and adjust with greater ease and success as you cross into unfamiliar territory.

It can be tempting to want to repeat familiar patterns of behavior and old ways of relating to others, even when these habits have not served you well. Remember, when you maintain an inquisitive spirit and learn to trust your intuition, you gain the insight needed to make healthier decisions for the future. The lessons harvested from your struggles offer opportunities to unlock your authentic self and live your life with purpose and meaning.

To learn from your struggles, you must connect with the silence within and reflect on what your hardships have to teach you. Ask yourself:

- What insights can I gain from my challenges?
- What am I to learn about the people, places and things in my life?
- What truths are they teaching me about who I am and my life's purpose?

At this moment, you may find yourself in the midst of tumult, navigating uncharted waters. Or you may be emerging from a deep, dark wood, finally able to make sense of your life journey. During these times of change, you must learn to trust the mystery of life's unfolding. When you awaken your courage and compassion, you discover the interrelatedness of your struggles.

Adversities offer opportunities to assess what really matters to you. Your soul is vast enough to hold the bounty of new vistas without abandoning the gifts harvested from past seasons. Believing tomorrow can be better fosters hope for today. As you courageously acknowledge the mystery of life's unfolding, you awaken your creativity and imagination to live your dreams and to explore all the infinite possibilities that await just over the horizon. In the midst of your life, you find the magic that makes your soul soar.

Life's Endings and Beginnings

THE LAWS OF THE NATURAL world remind us we are a part of the larger universe of continuous endings and beginnings. This transformational process is similar to the way the warmth of the sun and the gentle spring rains awaken the sleeping seed deep within the earth, calling it forth to bloom into its unique fullness and beauty. The journey of spiritual transformation through the dark night of the soul requires constantly pruning outlived beliefs and discarding broken dreams for new growth and goals that can ripen and flourish in this next stage of life.

Your decisions shape your destiny, in part. As French philosopher Jean-Paul Sartre advises, "You are your choices." Life is full of decisions. Some are momentous. Others may seem less significant, but are important nonetheless because they shape who you become. The freedom to have options and make decisions is actually a privilege of growth and transformation. Each choice you make that is aligned with your core beliefs is a deliberate step toward being who you truly are and living life more purposefully.

You can choose how you live your life despite any adversities you may face. On the one hand, you may fear looking at your struggles and choose to remain stuck in your pain rather than risk stepping onto "the road less traveled." On the other hand, you may feel excited and drawn to go in search of adventure. Regardless of whether you choose not to "rock the boat" or to risk stepping into a new frontier, your life changes, and you move right along with it. You can update the narrative of your story any time you make an intentional choice about how you want to live and how to use your unique gifts to make a difference.

When the decisions you make are grounded in your capacity to live aligned with purpose and passion, you fully participate in the world. Acting in the best interest of others contributes to creating unity with compassion. All of us have the agency to work for the greater good if we choose to use it. Your moral compass can help guide your choices and keep you moving toward your most passionate goals.

The answers to life are not revealed in true/false questions. *Nothing* is predestined or preordained. There is not a "best" solution or path, even if we spend years pondering the questions. Sometimes we spend so much time considering the possibilities and probabilities that we end up chasing our proverbial tail. We must take responsibility for our choices and make the best decision with as much insight as we can muster and then live with the outcome. Simply *choosing* is a step toward transformation.

The greatest act of embracing change is choosing to live according to these simple yet profound instructions:

- Make no judgments and have no expectations.
- Give up the need to know why things happen as they do.
- Trust that the unexpected events in your life are a form of spiritual awakening.
- Have the courage to make the decisions you need to make, accept what you cannot change, and be grateful for the wisdom to know the difference.

Endings play a necessary role in your quest for inner truth. Transitional wisdom teaches that you do not have to keep pain alive to allow truth to blossom. Trust that your suffering will diminish when you stop defining yourself by your woundedness and start loving who you truly are. By facing your fears and surrendering your need to control, you will ultimately experience joy and wonder.

You are free to choose how you want to live your life, deciding between desolation and hope, letting go of the old and creating a new vision for the future. Choose joy! Choose freedom! Choose delight! Choose to create the life you desire!

Soulful Self-Reflection: Finding Transitional Wisdom

Transitions demand courage and trust. If we're courageous enough to trust ourselves, then changes carry the possibility of spiritual growth and transformation. You may fail to recognize these opportunities if you don't first take time to ponder what you have lost or left behind. Doing this self-reflection will give you the confidence needed for life's unpredictable changes.

Find a quiet place and settle yourself. Begin by sitting and breathing gently, inhaling long and deep and then exhaling in a slow and relaxed manner. Allow yourself to be led to the silence within.

If at any time you lose focus or difficult emotions arise, simply acknowledge the sensations and bring your attention back to your breathing. Breathe gently and slowly, allowing your body to relax and be at peace.

Reflect on the questions below as they relate to a change you're currently facing. Then, write about those that resonate with you.

- What wisdom was revealed that will encourage me to pursue a new goal or create a vision for this next stage of my life?
- What choices could I make that would allow me to claim my authentic self and pursue my deepest values and passionate purpose?
- What is one decision that would move me a step closer to creating the life I desire and deserve?

Using the wisdom gained from this reflection, decide how you will implement a plan for living the life you envision with passion and purpose.

Transitional wisdom teaches you about the powerful threads of continuity that have guided your journey during the betwixt and between times, the endings and beginnings. The coping skills you refined during times of confusion and discontinuity are available throughout your lifetime, providing constant reassurance and knowledge. What comfort this offers as you welcome a new vision for the future!

Your Soul's Compass

THE JOURNEY OF LEARNING TO trust your soul is yours alone. No one else can walk it for you, and no one else can experience your inner knowing. Challenges force you to take a long, hard look at your life and ask yourself formative questions:

- Where do I fit into the world?
- What direction am I headed?
- How comfortable am I with how my life is going?

In the middle of a transition, you may not recognize where or who you are, or you may have forgotten what is central to your passion and purpose. To become aware of all the possibilities, you must acknowledge what you see and grieve for what you do not, relying on your spiritual DNA to guide you—your soul's compass.

In that moment of transformation, invite your spirit to lead you back to your true path. Welcome the deep wellspring of wisdom to bring light into the darkness and new direction to your journey. When you are conscious of the life you are living, you may realize you have barely experienced all the possibilities.

Awakening from the darkness involves shattering all your deep illusions and releasing all your fears of life's continuously changing landscape. When you're forced by circumstances to look deep below the surface, you'll discover new opportunities and adventures that align with your true path and your soul's passion and purpose.

Until you dig deep and walk through the darkness within, you will never know the joy of awakening. When you apply the insights gained from this effort, the surprises and unpredictability of life become the keys to spiritual growth and transformational wisdom.

 ## Soulful Self-Reflection: Learning from Your Life Journey

From time to time, it is important to slow your pace and ponder the question: "What has brought me to this place in my life?" Right here, right now, take a moment to reflect on your existence. This is the time and place to start paying attention to things as they truly are. There is no better occasion to begin wrestling with the deeper questions of life:

- Who am I now at this stage in my journey?
- What is my purpose?

- What gives my life meaning?
- How can I chart a vision for my future?

It may be surprising to learn that none of us could have predicted where we are today, with whom we have relationships, what careers we have held or abandoned, or our many successes and disappointments. If you don't reflect on your life at times, you will encounter some of the same difficult experiences and painful transitions. So, it is worthwhile to engage periodically in conscious self-reflection to learn from past events.

The first part of this exercise allows you to reflect on the experiences, events, people and places that have brought you to this moment, while the second part enables you to see how those have affected your life.

Find a quiet place and settle yourself. Begin by sitting and breathing gently, inhaling long and deep and then exhaling in a slow and relaxed manner. Allow yourself to be led to the silence within.

Think about your life journey. Celebrate the many events along the way, not just the high roads and the easy paths taken, but also the bumps in the road—the times you went off course or lost your way, needing new directions to get back on track. Be grateful for the roadblocks and obstacles you traversed, the breakdowns where you needed roadside assistance, the missed turns, and the dead ends. Reflect on the times the hills seemed too steep to climb and you questioned whether you could make it to the top, until you triumphantly reached the peak. Think about all the valleys, deep and dark, that seemed too frightening to enter, but where you pushed through, finally coming into the light with greater courage and confidence.

Consider the traveling companions you've met along the way who have inspired, encouraged and brought you joy, as well as those who inflicted heartache and pain. Who do you have by your side today? How are they contributing to your life? Imagine looking out the window at the current landscape. What do you see? Does the environment give you a deep sense of belonging?

Your life journey is yours alone, with all the unique experiences you have encountered and the hard-earned wisdom held in your memory. No one else on the planet has traveled this exact path. You would not be who you are today without each unforgettable experience and person you have known, without every place you have lived or explored on your travels, without all the exciting adventures and deep heartaches you have experienced.

Reflect on the questions below and write about those that resonate strongly for you. Let your thoughts, feelings and insights flow without explanation or worry about proper grammar or spelling. Remember to consider the significant highs and lows, triumphs celebrated, and obstacles overcome, and name the traveling companions who have affected your life.

Trust your inner voice as you contemplate these prompts:

- What have my experiences taught me about what gives my life purpose and meaning?
- What is my thread of continuity? What is the one belief or value that has remained constant throughout my life? How has that thread provided me with greater confidence and wisdom and kept me anchored during dark and stormy periods?
- What gifts of treasured wisdom are my constant source of hope, courage and comfort during turbulent transitions?
- Can I trust myself to make choices that align with the sacredness of my authentic self and purpose?
- What is the universe teaching me at this time? Am I open to it providing sacred wisdom for my journey?

Take time to cherish each memory as a vital component of the life story you're crafting every step you take. As you read back through what you've written, what insights did you gain?

Now, write about what you learned that has contributed to who you are today and provided you with purpose and meaning. Ask yourself:

Is it time to reset priorities and establish a new vision focused on hope and happiness?

When the world feels complicated and overwhelming, it may be a good time to pause and take a few moments to remind yourself of all the transitions that have contributed to the person you are today and helped you create the life you're living. Over the years, you have faced many pivotal moments, made numerous monumental decisions, and encountered significant people who have influenced your values and beliefs.

When you grasp the interconnectedness of life's endings and beginnings, you gain the courage to move beyond the present and begin your quest for wholeness—to know who you truly are and to claim your passion and purpose. With newfound courage and compassion, your soul senses the world that awaits you and awakens to exciting new possibilities that wait just over the horizon. Though your future is unknown, you step onto fresh ground with courage and delight, trusting the promise of new beginnings.

Chapter 10
Transforming Through Adversity

Watching the natural world reveals our relationship to the sacred realm. Change is constant. Things come and go, appear and disappear. If you walk outdoors, you will observe nature creating and growing every moment. Nothing is abrupt. Nothing is rushed. It insists on remaining faithful to the process until everything is ready to awaken into its unique fullness and beauty.

Too often, we try to gain a clear perspective before it is time or before we have enough information. We don't always know why things are happening the way they are or how a particular relationship will work out. Nor do we always understand why we feel a certain way, or what adjustments are needed, or why they're taking so long. What we are supposed to be learning from the present circumstances isn't always clear, nor do we understand how events will evolve and factor into the larger scheme of our life. We need time to accept that an ending is taking place and to reflect on the experiences that contributed to the transition.

The rhythm of change is a slow, laborious trek into uncharted territory. It takes time for whatever is being worked out to run its course and to clear away obstacles and create space for new people and places. Envisioning different opportunities and adventures requires space. Gaining a fresh perspective on what really matters requires an abundance of patience and perseverance. Trying to figure it all out today because we think we have all the answers or that we are in control is a waste of precious time and energy. We must have the courage to dig deep within ourselves and listen for the ongoing presence of our inner voice.

The journey is different for everyone. Transitions open you to a wide range of thoughts and feelings, including:

- discontent with your life or lifestyle, which may have provided happiness in years past, but no longer brings satisfaction
- boredom with people or things that previously interested you and dominated your life
- curiosity about new possibilities and a desire to do something completely different
- questions about the validity of your previous decisions
- confusion about where your life is headed
- uncertainty about your purpose and meaning in life

Just as the natural world needs room to grow to its full maturity, you can become stifled by your old routines, stuck in outlived goals, and suffocated by a lack of space to breathe and flourish. Transitions give you the space to review your current situation and evaluate which aspects to keep and which to let go.

You must claim all the different roles you play and the lives you share with others. As you establish a new level of awareness, examine your issues, discard any parts you've outlived, and update your inner truths. Allow time for reorientation and self-definition to take place and incorporate all the changes a life transition encompasses. Changes are ultimately an invitation to explore new people and places, to experience exciting opportunities for self-discovery, and to re-envision dreams for the future.

Struggles allow you to see the world in a new way by providing your greatest teaching moments. Discovering the wisdom of adversities begins by stepping into the sacred void and listening to the stirrings in the darkness. You may be surprised by what will arise from the silence within when you really listen to your inner voice and allow your questions to push you into the unknown.

Honor your courage as you move forward and trust the promise of new beginnings as you remember the constancy of the cyclical nature of life.

Unexpected Life-Altering Transitions

UNEXPECTED LIFE-ALTERING TRANSITIONS can knock us off balance, causing us to redefine who we are and to re-envision our life at this new stage. Let me share what I learned when my second husband, whom I was married to for twenty-five years, died suddenly.

My most vivid memory of that day of my husband's funeral is sitting on my couch with my dear friend, Dian, holding my hand as we waited for the limo to arrive and take us to the church. I remember saying, slowly and deliberately, "I don't know how to do this part!"

"How did you do it when your parents died?" Dian asked sympathetically.

My immediate thought was *Bud was there to support me, just as he had been throughout our marriage.* We had walked together through happy and turbulent times: our children's weddings, building our dream home, my doctoral program and internship, my neurosurgery, and the deaths of our parents. But now Bud was gone, and I had to figure out how to do life without him in it.

It all happened too fast. After Bud had a minor fender-bender, he was taken to the emergency room. Upon an initial examination, the doctor diagnosed him with terminal brain, lung and bone cancer. The test results showed Bud had possibly six months to live. The only treatment recommendation the doctors could make was radiation of the brain tumor to help relieve his pain and nausea. They ordered hospice care for him immediately after his release from the hospital. Bud lived for only three months.

I am grateful he did not suffer long, but for me, it happened much too quickly to even get my head around the fact that he had terminal cancer. The few weeks we had after his diagnosis only allowed brief moments to process our life together and say our final goodbyes. Now, as I look back over the months prior to his death, I recognize the changes in his personality, physical functioning, and cognitive abilities were because of the cancer that had devastated his body long before that life-altering diagnosis.

Part of what made it devastating was how unexpected it was and the fact that it felt like we were living full and rich lives. Bud had taken early retirement as a university professor and environmental scientist to expand his private consulting business in water ecology. We had just completed building our dream home on the 183-acre property we both loved. Our children were raised, living independently and making their own life plans to our delight and enjoyment. My clinical practice was going well. We were living our dream, with the prospect of new adventures together.

The days and weeks following Bud's death remain somewhat of a blur, even today. Making funeral arrangements, taking care of the legal procedures, and getting through the memorial services took all my energy and emotional stamina. My family and closest friends were a constant source of support and comfort. But when everyone returned to their homes, when all the visitors stopped bringing casseroles and condolences, and when the heartfelt phone calls and sympathy cards stopped arriving, I was left to begin my grief journey alone. My quest for a new vision was mine to chart; no one else could map this new course but me.

All the books written about the grief process tell us that the journey is long and arduous. The first year is often challenging because of all the "firsts" that must be mourned—the first holidays, the first birthdays, the first anniversaries, the first time attending a previously shared event or special occasion all alone. With each "first," our new painful reality is brought to our attention, forcing us to mourn that particular stepping-stone.

When someone incredibly close to us dies, we feel their loss on a deep and fundamental level. When we lose our parents, we lose our past, with all the memories they alone held from the moment we entered this world. If our child dies, we lose hope that our dreams for them will become a reality. If we lose our spouse or life partner, we lose our witness to the most intimate details of our daily life.

The pure essence of our loved one must be mourned and remembered. The way their nose wrinkled when they laughed. Their gentle, reassuring hugs. The soothing sound of their calming voice. All their quirky jokes, their idiosyncrasies and mannerisms that brought a smile to everyone's face. Their personal characteristics, gifts and talents. Even the things that used to drive us nuts about them now bring a smile and a shake of the head. The distinct peculiarities, irritating habits, and amazing qualities that made them special and unique are all lost with them and must be mourned. Losing the joy of their presence must be grieved. No one else can ever occupy that special space in our life or hold all our shared memories.

Following the tragedy of 9/11, Queen Elizabeth II is said to have comforted the world with these poignant words: "Grief is the price we pay for love." We honor our dear one by holding our love for them in our heart forever.

Throughout the first year following Bud's death, I kept returning to my original statement: "I don't know how to do this part!" I knew how to do my professional life, but my personal life was a mystery. My work provided stability and grounding as I navigated the uncharted territory of becoming a widow. My grief journey centered on the transformational questions "Who am I now at this new stage in my life?" and "What do I want and need to make a new vision for myself?"

The wisdom I gained from the death of my husband has been transformative. I learned that grief is a healing process. There are different phases, and each has its own purpose. Because every journey is unique, there is no clearly defined roadmap and no pat answers to the recurring questions: "How long will my grief last?" "How do I get through it?" "Will I ever be myself again?" Here are some truths I learned that continue to provide me comfort and assurance that you may find helpful.

I discovered that when I allowed myself solitude and patience to accept and express my feelings, the frequency and intensity of my emotions lessened over time. A positive outcome of my healing process is that I am a more resilient, self-assured, courageous and empathetic person. Having a new perspective on what is truly important in my life, I have the confidence to make positive choices in my best interest to create the future I desire.

Grief's gifts are available to anyone who courageously seeks to unravel their own truths. The cyclical nature of life guarantees there will always be times when everything seems to be turned upside down and we must begin healing again. Knowing others have faced similar devastating losses and found comfort and wisdom helps to instill hope for and faith in a brighter tomorrow.

Soulful Self-Reflection: Finding the Purpose in Everything

Elisabeth Kübler-Ross wisely wrote, "Learn to get in touch with the silence within yourself and know that everything in this life has a purpose, there are no mistakes, no coincidences, all events are blessings given to us to learn from."[57] Silence beckons us to slow down and trust that time spent amid adversities will ultimately reveal exciting new possibilities for a brighter tomorrow. Now is the time to be still and listen to your inner voice.

When you undergo a major turning point and life changes dramatically, it is not uncommon to experience an identity crisis. In this meditation, you will reflect on a time when everything shifted and you questioned: "Who am I now? And what is this transition teaching me?" Allow this exercise to help you delve deep within to retrieve the lessons learned and insights gained because of what happened.

Find a quiet place and settle yourself. Close your eyes and place one hand lightly over your heart. Rest the other gently on your belly. Allow your breath to go deep into your diaphragm, drop your shoulders, unclench your teeth, and relax your jaw. Simply notice your breathing until the intervals between become slow and relaxed. Allow yourself to be led to the silence within.

Reflect on the questions below and write about the ones that resonate strongly for you. Let your thoughts, feelings and insights flow without explanation or concern about proper grammar or spelling. Trust your inner voice as you consider these prompts:

- What events or crises occurred that forced me to look at life differently?
- How did I adapt to that adversity?

---

57 Elisabeth Kübler-Ross Foundation, "Quotes," *Elisabeth Kübler-Ross Foundation*, accessed July 1, 2025, emeraldlakebooks.com/ntkublerross.

- What wisdom did I gain as a result of that transition?
- How can I make peace with life's ever-changing landscape and accept that everything that happens is part of my journey?

Transformation is not only about letting go of what has been lost. It includes considering questions like the ones above and integrating what you learn into your life journey. Wholeness and healing are possible when you patiently take time to find meaning in your adversities. It is only then that acceptance can bring peace to your soul, when you realize everything has a purpose.

The Heroic Quest for Wholeness

MANY OF THE WORLD'S MYTHIC JOURNEYS involve remembering who we are and discovering our unique purpose. This search, though often unacknowledged, is what sustains and guides our journey of transformation.

The quest requires awakening and connecting with the wisdom that dwells deep within your soul—the spiritual center of your being and the place where you are most yourself. Only when you achieve an intimacy with your authentic self do you become aware of your true nature, your deepest desires, and your unique gifts, passions and purpose. This knowledge will enable you to create the life you long for.

Every culture and spiritual tradition contemplates these universal questions:

- Who am I?
- What is my passion? And my purpose?
- What are the unique gifts I bring to the world?
- What legacy do I want to leave behind when I'm gone?
- Can I look back on my life with peace, knowing I have lived purposefully and meaningfully?

These questions often surface during crises, when your standard answers no longer satisfy. Your deepest longing is to find creative harmony with your authentic self and to align with your purpose. It wounds your soul to act in a way that inhibits your quest for wholeness. To live authentically is to live a limitless life. Your search requires being open to the mystery of what lies ahead.

We all seek experiences of joy, happiness and fulfillment, which create a sense of security and well-being. But life is not always conducive to happiness and joy. There will be betrayals, losses and tragedies that rob you of your peace. When bad things happen, these wounds leave psychological scars that can become internalized as the stirrings of doubt, shame and guilt. This is not your true voice. It is society telling you who you are expected to become because of your woundedness. If you listen to what others have to say, you lose touch with your authentic self.

Within you lies two parts of your true nature: your ideal version of how you want to present yourself to the world, and what Carl Jung described as "the shadow"—aspects of yourself you dislike, refuse to see, and seek to hide. The shadow is part of your unconscious, intended to seek pleasure and avoid pain. It is made up of your primal instincts and urges.

You were not born with this shadow. You unwittingly constructed it at a young age to curb your natural impulses and desires in order to have your needs met and evade punishment. Without the necessary impulse control or language to express your needs, your behaviors became your primary mode of communication. However, temper tantrums, pouting or stomping off in anger only served to irritate and displease others. Fear of rejection, disapproval or abandonment may have led to a pattern of pleasing people, being "good," or not wanting to upset others.

As you matured, it's possible you lost touch with your natural impulses, emotions, instincts and desires out of a need to be loved and accepted. Your true nature may be so well hidden you might not even see the wild complexity of who you genuinely are—the beauty of your authentic self.

As an adult, whenever you encounter a stressful situation and feel trapped or under duress, you might respond by becoming confused or defensive, crying, pouting, lashing out, or withdrawing. These behaviors are the shadow aspects you may want to disown, but that are reenacted as old patterns of relating to others, which negatively affect your relationships and interfere with the ability to express your true nature.

Discernment is an essential tool for you to use when unmasking your shadow. You can begin the process by observing yourself in stressful situations. How do you react to conflict, disappointment and loss? When you're triggered, what mask do you put on?

By setting healthy boundaries, you can confront your shadow by taking responsibility for your inappropriate or overly emotional responses. You can effectively communicate your thoughts and feelings, set appropriate limits, and respectfully advocate for your needs and desires. With discernment, you are able to change how you act and react, and claim your true nature, allowing a more congruent and honest expression of your authentic self.

When you honor who you truly are, you no longer need to worry that no one will love you if you show them your true self. You do not have to worry someone will reveal any lack of self-worth you may feel, tell you who you need to be for their sake, or what you can do to make them happy. By letting go of your pain, you allow your inner truth to blossom. As you recognize your self-worth and trust your wisdom, you allow your natural instincts and intuition to help guide your heroic quest for wholeness.

When you have the courage to detach from past difficulties with compassion and empathy, you become aware of how your life transitions have shaped who you are. Detaching from your shadow enables you to recognize aspects of your true nature that you may have unconsciously ignored or disregarded. Facing it conquers your fear of exposure, freeing you to be your authentic self. No longer defining yourself by your woundedness allows you to gain a strength-based identity: I *am* resilient. I *am* courageous. I *am* worthy of love.

When you let go and gently ease into your authentic self, you realize you are embraced by a life that is larger and more abundant than you ever imagined. You begin to accept adversities not as tragedies or failures, but rather as lessons containing wisdom to be claimed. You discover true joy and peace. When you befriend your shadow, you are free to discover your true nature and become your undivided, authentic self.

The Art of Claiming Your True Self

A̶ccepting your strengths and weaknesses, successes and failures, as well as the events that have played a part in your life, is to know your worth and love yourself unconditionally. When you recognize your courage and strength, your resilience and stamina, you honor the person you are today. Compassion for yourself allows forgiveness and acceptance to enter your soul, and you begin to see your story differently. Knowing you will never fully understand why things happen as they do, you can look at yourself with a humble attitude of acceptance and compassion.

Self-compassion means being kind and understanding toward yourself, rather than being self-critical. It results in your claiming your achievements and successes together with your regrets and failures. As you cultivate this perspective, you learn to treat yourself with respect, honesty and love, and you embody those qualities in all your relationships. This enables you to accept others without trying to change them to meet your needs.

To love and be loved requires giving and receiving without judgment or expectation. When you trust your inner truth and self-worth, you experience more joy and creative energy. You can be more relaxed and peaceful, taking pleasure in what might unfold to your delight and surprise.

As you acknowledge a shift in your consciousness, you gain the gifts of self-knowledge, confidence and courage, and you become aware of how the transformational process reveals a greater sense of purpose. As you embrace your wisdom, your actions align with your values and beliefs, and you orient toward a deeper peace and unity with the world. You have faith that all is unfolding according to divine timing, and you are exactly where you are supposed to be. As you move into a new phase of your journey, you recognize that, even in the midst of turmoil and suffering, you have gained wisdom and added depth to your life.

Most importantly, when you strip away the layers of lies and pretenses in your quest for wholeness and get down to the wild flow of energy in the well of your soul, you claim the beauty of your authentic self. You experience the freedom to sing your own song, dance your own dance, and speak your own truth without fear or hesitation.

Medieval philosopher Meister Eckhart, a celebrated spiritual leader for more than eight centuries, wrote that within each of us is a divine treasure, and if we hope to discover it, we need to go deep into the heart of who we are. As spiritual beings, we are born with a "little spark," as Eckhart called it, that belongs entirely to spirit.⁵⁸ Like a diamond sparkling in the sunshine, your authentic self has always been there, unchangeable and untouched by illusion.⁵⁹ When you step into the light, you see the wild complexity and beauty of who you truly are.

Soulful Self-Reflection: Digging For Treasure in the Ashes

The art of claiming your true self is not a horizontal shift in the conscious mind from one way of thinking to another, but rather a vertical descent into the darkness of your soul to shine a light on the treasure of your authentic self. This inner journey is similar to the ancient practice of alchemy—employing fire to change metal into gold. Using this metaphor, inner alchemy is the process of releasing your true self from the unrefined, outdated aspects of yourself that have fulfilled their purpose and are no longer needed.

The toughest part is descending deep within with a courageous heart, naming the darkness for what it is and relinquishing to the fire what is unnecessary. This transformative process begins when you bravely ask, "What is it that I need right here and now to turn rust into gold?"

In this meditation, I invite you to enter the darkness. There, you will sift through and name your feelings, thoughts and beliefs, and let the ones that no longer serve you "burn" in a healing flame of renewal. Then, to grasp your inner truths, you must muster the courage to dig through the ashes and uncover the gifts of wisdom left behind.⁶⁰ These insights become the guiding light leading you to claim the treasure of your authentic self.

---

58 Jon M. Sweeney and Mark S. Burrows, *Meister Eckhart's Book of Darkness & Light: Meditations on the Path of the Wayless Way* (Hampton Roads Publishing Company, Inc., 2023), 102.

59 Richard Rohr, *Immortal Diamond: The Search for Our True Self* (Jossey-Bass, 2013), 38–39.

60 Douglas-Klotz, *Hidden Gospel*, 143–144.

Find a quiet place and settle yourself. Close your eyes and place one hand lightly over your heart. Rest the other gently on your belly. Allow your breath to go deep into your diaphragm, drop your shoulders, unclench your teeth, and relax your jaw. Simply notice your breathing until the intervals between become slow and relaxed.

Bring your awareness into the darkness of your inner being. Visualize a fire burning brightly inside you. See all the parts clearly: the bright flame, the glowing light, and the shimmering wave of heat.

Acknowledge everything deep inside that feels chaotic, rigid, painful, outdated or no longer essential. It is time to relinquish the obsolete facets of your identity or reality to the fire. Name each aspect you wish to discard—your old fears, illusions, rigidity, regrets, hurt, shame and guilt—and relinquish it to the flames. Imagine the negative, outlived beliefs and self-destructive patterns burning away in the blaze.

You can transform these shattered pieces into treasure. Digging through the debris uncovers the gifts of self-respect, self-compassion, empathy and unconditional positive regard for what is truly precious and vital. Acknowledge these gifts and allow them to merge with your true self. Then, give thanks for the journey that has revealed the wisdom of who you truly are.

Use these prompts to help unearth the treasures of your authentic self:

- What obsolete parts of my identity or past reality did I discard and let burn in the fire?
- What outlived, irrational beliefs or self-destructive patterns did I relinquish to the flames?
- What treasures did I uncover by digging in the ashes?
- Did merging these gifts into myself allow me to heal? If so, how?

After you have finished responding to these questions, write freely about whatever feelings, thoughts and insights were retrieved from the ashes. Acknowledge how these gifts will allow you to claim the beauty and joy of who you were born to be as you move forward. Stop when you feel your writing is complete.

When you bravely descend into the depths of your darkness and wait patiently with an open heart, something mysterious happens. You experience an awakening of your authentic self—your trusted companion on your heroic quest for wholeness.

Chapter 11
Exploring Passion, Purpose and New Territory

No life is easy, and things will not always be the way you hoped they would be. When monumental tragedies disrupt your center of gravity, you may feel as though you are dangling by a thread, without solid grounding to hold you in place. You may experience what St. John of the Cross referred to as "the dark night of the soul." When you feel you have lost your way and life is devoid of meaning and purpose, you may lose faith in yourself and in life itself. Your desire and ability to move forward are drastically tested. During these momentous times, something within must arise to keep you grounded, to help you survive. Find the spiritual resilience to keep moving forward.

During life's greatest challenges and overwhelming tragedies, it is paramount to search for meaning and purpose. If you fail to do the hard inner work of transforming adversity into wisdom, you risk losing the most meaningful part of your journey. The questions you must answer are: "When facing a crossroad, how does my purpose and meaning guide me?" and "How can I find a passion for living once again?"

We are not here on earth accidentally, nor are we meant to remain neutral when difficulties arise. You are a spiritual being born with a seed of selfhood that not only determines who you are but contains your unique gifts, your complex passions, and all the characteristics distinct to your purpose. One of the greatest challenges is to discover your passion and your unique aspirations that are in harmony with your true self. Once you do this, life takes on a focus that unites you with the rhythm of your soul's deepest longing. Never finding your purpose can become a burden that leads to continual restlessness and dissatisfaction.

Your passion may remain hidden deep within your soul in your natural talents, instincts, interests, aptitudes or desires. From an early age, you might have had a deep longing to be a scientist, an artist, a parent, an educator, a caregiver, an architect, a chef—the list goes on and on. Over time, your purpose may unfold organically into an inner knowing: *This is what I am called to do!* That knowledge may begin as a soft whisper that eventually grows louder and louder into a persistent stirring that is almost impossible to ignore. You may try to silence it or push it away, but it can't be hushed.

If a nudge is not enough, a loud scream may be necessary to get your attention. Your soul will do whatever is needed to pursue its passion. Your purpose may change over time and look different as your circumstances evolve and you reach new phases in life. What remains the same is that when you find what feeds your soul, you focus on making changes. True joy comes when you use your unique gifts, passions and purpose to make a difference in your little corner of the world.

Do you recall Alexis's story about her transformational choice? During the final three months of her mother's life, they shared deep conversations focused on the goals they had accomplished, the dreams they had ignored, and her mother's remembrance of how much Alexis had loved making art. Alexis had put it aside and made a different career choice to fulfill what she believed were the expectations of others. After her mother's death, Alexis tried to deny the feeling that her current job had no "spark" as well as her longings for creative and fulfilling work. But her inner stirrings could not be silenced. The adage "Some jobs feed the belly, and some jobs feed the soul" describes her situation. She listened, bravely quit her job, and began taking art classes. Today, she is an internationally known artist and art educator. Her courageous choice to follow her heart continues to feed her soul, and new dreams unfold to her delight and pleasure. When your natural talents converge with your passion and purpose, your chosen vocation can fulfill you, and you discover the joy of living in harmony with your truest self.

Only a few people are born with the natural talent to become a world-famous musician or win a Nobel Peace Prize or discover the cure for cancer. But each of us is born with unique gifts that we bring to the world. They are part of our spiritual DNA, a part of us that never changes. We express our passion and purpose through acts of kindness, friendship, joy, patience, service, hope, peace, love and many others. What we say and do, and how we treat others, matters. Being compassionate and caring is purpose. Volunteering at a local food bank is purpose. Tutoring an elementary student who has difficulty reading is purpose. Delivering meals to housebound seniors is purpose. Sharing a kind word or simply smiling at someone who might be going through a tough time is purpose. "Paying it forward" serves all humankind. You are free every moment to use your gifts to make a difference in the lives of others.

Many people transform tragedies into making a positive difference by searching for their inner fire. The national nonprofit group Sandy Hook Promise is an example of how victims of gun violence turned their anger and anguish into action. Sandy Hook Promise was founded and is led by families whose loved ones were killed in a mass school shooting at Sandy Hook Elementary School in Newtown, CT. The nonprofit allows these families to rally around a cause they believe in, which helps them feel the loss of their loved ones isn't in vain. Their mission is to advocate for education and legislation in the fight for gun safety and to empower others to prevent violence in schools, homes and communities, making schools across the country safer and kinder. Sandy Hook Promise demonstrates how we all can bring goodness, and even greatness, into the world. Life's darkest tragedies can soften our hearts, and we can become more compassionate toward ourselves and others.

Suffering is a necessary ingredient for developing compassion and inner strength. We can overcome immense struggle and emerge eager to spread good in the world. Enduring our own challenges helps us become willing to listen to the struggles of others. They, too, are human beings molded by tragedy. Our "broken places" allow us to see the world from a broader perspective. When you are struggling, ask yourself: "How can I use this experience as an opportunity to gain wisdom? How can I transmute my perspective from a negative one into a way of expressing compassion and love?"

Compassion is an essential part of your true nature, and you need it most during challenging times. It comes from the Latin words *cum patior*, meaning to suffer with. Both recognition and sorrow are integral to true compassion. Having compassion requires an ability to embrace all of humanity and to allow your interior life to reflect the pains and joys of all people. Compassion means perceiving adversity as a part of the larger human experience, rather than seeing it as an isolated moment that interrupts peace.

When you know your true self and your unique gifts, you develop a sense of compassionate engagement and social responsibility that is bigger than yourself. His Holiness the Dalai Lama has been telling us for years, "If you want others to be happy, practice compassion. If you want to be happy, practice compassion." Cultivating this skill teaches you how to enter into your own intense emotions, where you gain the insight and understanding needed to extend love and compassion to others who are suffering. When you search inward and listen wholeheartedly to your inner voice, you discover the inspiration and passion to transform yourself and your world.

Overcoming struggle and emerging with a compassionate heart develops an appreciation for the joyfulness of life. Joy can arise from sadness, and a new beginning can emerge from chaos and confusion. Awakening joy is a way to live a meaningful and purposeful life. Being joyful helps you let go of fear and uncertainty so you can move forward into the future with confidence and courage, and trust that a new vision will unfold organically.

Purpose lives where passion resides—where joy thrives. When life dramatically changes and you are forced to look at circumstances differently, you must learn to be surprised by joy, your own resilience, and your courage to grow and change. Be thrilled by the new opportunities and possibilities you never could have imagined that lie just over the horizon. Let the knowledge of what you desire and what gives your life passion and purpose excite you. Be amazed by the joy of knowing you are changing and entering into a new beginning.

Joy is a way of *being*, not just feeling. True joy comes from engaging in something bigger than yourself that contributes to the good of others. When you awaken its beauty within your soul, you bring light wherever you go. In this powerful transformation, you become the embodiment of joy and love, linked to compassion for all humanity.

In his poem "Last Night As I Was Sleeping," Spanish poet Antonio Machado writes about a dream he had where bees were making "sweet honey from my old failures."[61]

When circumstances have broken us, their "sweet honey" can become the nectar for a new beginning. Imagine the marvelous possibilities when you accept that everything that happens is not wasted. Even your darkest moments can become the raw material for tasting the sweetness of life.

As you acknowledge and accept change as a vital part of the journey, the invisible is revealed and something magical happens—you find meaning and purpose even in the most tragic adversities. This does not mean that your suffering is diminished, that things become any easier, or that your struggles and pain are taken away. Your path will still be marred by traumatic events, and your transformation may still be a long, arduous journey of self-discovery. You learn life may *not* be about avoiding the bruises. Maybe it's about collecting scars to prove you showed up.

When your life seems to have crumbled into tiny pieces, when you descend all the way to the depths of your self, that is when you are open to the possibility of spiritual transformation. As you become honest with yourself, you are able to trust the healing wisdom within your soul. As you gain peace with your story and allow self-love to enter your being, you begin to live life with passion and purpose. These are the hard-earned gifts of wisdom and enlightenment, which help sustain hope for and faith in a brighter tomorrow during the treachery of transition.

Believing your tomorrows can be more fulfilling and meaningful fosters hope for today. Claiming your courage, you discover the beginning of a new vision for yourself. The gift of life is given to you to bring joy, love and compassion to others. Grant yourself permission to claim your true self and live wholeheartedly with passion and purpose.

---

61 Antonio Machado, "Last Night As I Was Sleeping," trans. Robert Bly, in *Ten Poems to Change Your Life*, ed. Roger Housden (Harmony Books, 2001), 20–21; originally published in *Times Alone: Selected Poems of Antonio Machado*, trans. Robert Bly (Wesleyan University Press, 1983).

Soulful Self-Reflection: Living with Passion and Purpose

Honest soul-searching in the midst of the unpredictable trials you've been through helps you discover your meaning and purpose. When you understand life's vicissitudes, your consciousness is enlarged, and you emerge from the dark woods into the light. Your passion and purpose restore harmony with your sacred self and with the world. You must find your path through the darkness on your quest to live your life wholeheartedly.

In this meditation, I will guide you as you breathe light into your soul and claim your unique spiritual identity: who you are, as well as your strengths, gifts, passions and purpose. Then, you will commit to pursuing a goal that will bring meaning to your life.

Find a quiet place and settle yourself. Close your eyes and place one hand lightly over your heart. Rest the other gently on your belly. Allow your breath to go deep into your diaphragm, drop your shoulders, unclench your teeth, and relax your jaw. Simply notice your breathing until the intervals between become slow and relaxed. Allow yourself to be led to the silence within.

Now, imagine a bright light shining over your head. Picture your breath bringing it gently and slowly down from the crown of your skull throughout your body. Feel the refreshing air and vibrant glow that are your connection with the spark that contains your unique purpose, which is whole and complete.

As you hold these thoughts and feelings, focus on an image or symbol that represents a specific goal or purpose you have for your life. Imbue this icon with your wholehearted commitment. Expand your consciousness to include all the possible ways you can make this goal a reality.

Write your answers to the questions below that resonate strongly with you. Let your thoughts, feelings and insights flow without explanation or concern about proper grammar or spelling. Trust your inner voice as you consider these prompts:

- Which unique gifts are an expression of my purpose and passion?

- What image or symbol emerged that represents a specific goal I have for my life?
- What is one thing I can commit to pursuing that would bring me closer to my dreams, desires and goals for the future?
- How will I allow the wisdom of my infinite spark to guide my journey?

Once you've finished reflecting on those questions, ask yourself: "Does my purpose have heart?" and "Does it contain the desire to engage enthusiastically in what I am passionate about?"

Fulfilling your life purpose has enormous healing power. When you can express your birthright nature, which contains the gifts you alone bring to the world, your soul will be filled with gratitude. Realize all the good you can do that will bring joy and comfort to the world.

The Threshold Into New Territory

THE TRANSFORMATIONAL JOURNEY ENTAILS a succession of new thresholds to cross. A threshold is not a simple boundary to be stepped over. It is an in-between place that divides a familiar territory and an unfamiliar frontier. This space is where the tension between who we are and who we can become lives. Crossing into new territory can be challenging, and it creates emotional uncertainty. It is in these transitional moments of your life that authentic transformation can happen if you are willing to leave your comfort zone and risk stepping into the unknown.

When you focus on the future rather than allowing the past to consume your mind, body and spirit, you discover that adversities have the potential to bring about your greatest moments of creativity. Your wounds will bear the fruits of courage and confidence, resilience and resourcefulness. What seems to be an ending becomes a new beginning. What seems to be a tragedy becomes a cause for courage. What seems to be a failure can become a triumph. And what seems to be a cause for despair can become a moment of hope.

You cannot predict with clarity what lies ahead. All you can do is trust that the future will unfold organically and you will gain the gifts of transformational wisdom when you cross the threshold into a new territory.

As you explore new possibilities and examine new priorities, you rediscover personal traits, such as curiosity, adventure and creativity, that you thought had disappeared, creating surprise and delight. These traits are lifelong gifts that enhance your well-being and play an important role in your overall mental, physical and spiritual health. They are key elements of our humanity that exist in everyone, at any age, regardless of how much or little you use or consciously recognize them. It is never too late to tap into these renewable and vibrant resources.

To experience living with gratitude, learn to exercise curiosity and creativity. As they blossom, you gain clarity that deepens your longing for feeling at home with yourself. When you see your life as alive with possibilities, you are released from the darkness into the light of hope for a brighter tomorrow. Find the courage to listen to your inner voice and to wait patiently for a new vision to ripen and unfold. Trust that space will open for creating the life your soul seeks.

During an interview with the journalist Bill Moyers, mythologist Joseph Campbell was asked about his thoughts on our search for meaning in life. Campbell responded:

> I think what we're seeking is an experience of being alive, so that the life experiences that we have on the purely physical plane will have resonances within, that are those of our own innermost being and reality. And so that we actually feel the rapture of being alive.[62]

When you are tested, your faith and confidence can deepen and gratitude can fill your heart. After making it through life's darkest storms, you discover that even your most difficult moments can bring an appreciation for the gift of life itself.

---

62 Originally aired on public television on May 30, 1988. This transcript was published on billmoyers.com on October 17, 2014. A Production of Public Affairs Television and Alvin H. Permutter, Inc. 1988.

Soulful Self-Reflection: Enjoying the Rapture of Being Alive

Transitions teach you to savor life. It is only by diving deep into the darkness of your emotions that you discover what Joseph Campbell called "the rapture of being alive." You may fail to recognize the possibilities for growth and transformation because you neglect thinking about them in a thoughtful and nuanced way. Take the time for self-reflection to gain the confidence and wisdom needed during tenuous transitions.

Your task in this meditation is to dig deep within for wisdom about what matters most to you. These new insights offer an opportunity to reexamine and reset your priorities to align with your true values, and they allow you to gain a deep appreciation for the life you are living.

Find a quiet place and settle yourself. Close your eyes and place one hand lightly over your heart. Rest the other gently on your belly. Allow your breath to go deep into your diaphragm, drop your shoulders, unclench your teeth, and relax your jaw. Simply notice your breathing until the intervals between become slow and relaxed. If at any time you lose focus or difficult emotions arise, simply acknowledge the sensations and bring your attention back to your breathing.

Reflect on the questions below. Write about a transition in your life that resonates strongly with you. Let your thoughts, feelings and insights flow without explanation or concern about proper grammar or spelling. Trust your inner voice as you consider these prompts:

- Which difficult situation or tumultuous transition has ultimately delivered the gift of gratitude?
- What holds me back from surrendering and claiming the "rapture of being alive?"

After reflecting on these questions, formulate a plan for what to do based on these new insights.

> Life's greatest challenges demand radical resilience to overcome the pain and suffering you experience when circumstances change and you realize nothing is the same. Real heroism requires absolute faithfulness to your authentic path by not allowing adversities to stop you from living abundantly with passion and purpose.
>
> Encounters with anguish, despair and darkness can open your heart to an awareness of immense gratitude for the simple gift of life. Discovering who you truly are brings the treasured gifts of delight, inner knowing and the "rapture of being alive."

Jessi's Grit and Grace

Here's a story of my friend Jessi's journey to find purpose through loss and determination.

I have lived my life with grit and grace, and I am so thankful for having both. It is only in looking back at my life and career that I can see how powerfully both were at work. It's clear to me now how the moments of sadness, loss, terror, hopelessness and perceived helplessness collided with grace and gave me a life full of wonderful people and a sense of purpose I thought I never would have. Had I given up at any of the million "intersections" I arrived at, I would not know the joy and satisfaction of a career and life fully lived.

I was a first-generation college student who, against all odds, later became the vice president for student affairs at a university. When I was in school, I didn't have the time or resources to fully appreciate all the things being offered at that institution. Yet, I still finished my bachelor's degree.

I applied to graduate school for a program I had no interest in because I was told it was the next logical step. When I was rejected, I thought my academic career was over. Little did I know, it saved my life. I was able to change direction, take a risk, and apply to a different program that I believed would give me the sense of purpose I so desperately wanted.

After I graduated with my master's degree, an old youth leader from my church told me about an opening for a counselor at a university on the other side of the state. I had never considered a college setting as a career direction, but I applied and got the job.

On a beautiful sunny day, walking across campus, I believed I heard the voice of God telling me this was to be my life. This was not quite a "burning bush" moment, but I understood the message and believed in the Messenger. I had found my purpose. After five years, I knew I wanted more, so I went back to graduate school.

My doctoral program and work at the university were the most difficult yet important pursuits of my career. I learned so many lessons, both in and out of the classroom. They all would eventually shape how I led, listened to, and cared for staff and students in my charge.

Like getting old, working in student affairs isn't for sissies. It is challenging, exhausting and sometimes terrifying and sad. Sexual violence, mental health crises, protests, suicide, alcohol and drug issues, discrimination, accidents and other mayhem were unfortunately routine.

In addition to my studies and work, I also had a two-year encounter with a stalker. He threatened my life numerous times. Back then, stalking laws did not exist in Arizona, making meaningful prosecution impossible. It was simply terrifying. Grit kept me going, and grace kept me alive.

I received my doctorate and became an academic traveler of sorts, moving east and north and then back to the center of the country. I ended my career at Oklahoma State University (OSU).

The lessons I learned at OSU were often difficult, but every experience allowed me to strengthen my knowledge, skills, compassion and prayer life. The terrorist attack on 9/11, two plane crashes that affected our university community, and a car driven by a mentally ill woman who destroyed the lives of homecoming parade attendees (four people died and forty-four were injured, some critically) were among the most memorable crises I dealt with.

Every day, there were students who needed immediate assistance, direction and care, and I was able to help. There were budget cuts, staff reductions, difficult political situations, challenging people, and exhausting schedules.

I remember some incidents with remarkable clarity, and others are foggy reminders of past stressors. What I will always remember are the people who stepped forward to help in a crisis, those that took the time to make a difference when it mattered most. What a privilege it was to serve!

In January 2019, I retired after forty-two years in higher education. Looking back, I see that, during challenging times, I had what I needed to survive and even thrive. The things I feared the most when I was twenty (being alone, moving and starting over, not finding my purpose) melted away with time and experience.

Taking risks, trusting I would find what I needed wherever my journey took me, and receiving an abundance of grace led me to and through my career. I now volunteer as a patient advocate in the emergency room at our hospital. I guess I missed the lights and sirens.

Transitions, including retirement, are hard, but if we don't keep moving and looking for the opportunities to serve others, life loses significance.

Along the way, we're going to experience both highs and lows. But when we live from our passion and purpose, we can appreciate just how truly amazing life is, no matter what the circumstance.

The Promise of New Beginnings

LIFE IS A SUCCESSION OF endings and beginnings. That is the promise of the natural world—a continual cycle of joy and sadness. We can only try to find the words to explain our deep and complex emotions around this. Our hearts can be filled with perfect joy while knowing sadness will come from that same deep place within. Without the storms of life, we will never know peace and wholeness. Living within the paradox of enduring the "dark night of the soul" while abiding in our peace is a constant struggle. Even the darkest storms carry the promise of new beginnings.

At the center of your human suffering, there is a peaceful, enduring space where your soul dwells. It does not seek answers; instead, it seeks meaning. As the spiritual center of your being, your soul is the place where you are your truest self. It is present within you every moment and knows that anger, sadness and anxiety are part of the transformational process. Stressful circumstances may dim its energy, but they won't snuff it out. Even in your darkest hour, when all seems lost, if you are willing to search for the blessing of the wisdom the storm brings, your wounds will be healed and you will be granted peace.

Your soul does whatever it can to keep you on your journey to embrace change. It seeks truth and will ultimately reveal your true self and purpose. Inner revelation fortifies your soul and provides courage and fosters commitment to remain open to life's changing landscape, despite all your pain, sorrow and human frailty. You must embrace change, however much it hurts, and accept that what is happening in your life is true, inevitable and ultimately will teach you transitional wisdom. When you remain open to your soul's inner truth, it will support you as you navigate toward wholeness.

By trusting your wisdom, you find a balance between living in the present and intentionally searching inward for a new vision. Even if the destination is unclear, the promise of new beginnings emerges through the voyage into the unknown. When you move forward with intention and perseverance, you come to honor your own tenacity and the courage that deepens your faith in what lies ahead. This inner strength opens the door to fresh opportunities for growth. In facing adversity, you begin to chart a path toward healing and wholeness.

When your heart is ready for a fresh beginning, your soul senses it is time to relinquish its grip on the past and risk the new horizon that awaits. Oftentimes, your inner voice may be no louder than a heartbeat, so you must listen closely and constantly. You may be surprised by what it reveals. Even the act of hearing your soul may be a signal that there is more to life than you imagined. It may call, "Are you ready for the next big adventure?"

Now is the time to let go and just "be." Let go of the need to figure it all out, the need to fix things, the illusion of control… You must release earlier hurts, betrayals, anger, heartaches and hardships. Don't allow your thoughts to be consumed by going down the old paths that destroy your joy. Resist the urge to hang on to the past and pry yourself away from things that hold you back or need to be left behind. Surrendering may result in making some difficult adjustments together with taking some unexpected adventures. To experience the joy of peace, you must shed your anxieties, fears and preoccupations. When you allow your natural instincts, intuitions and creative energy to unfold rather than clinging to your preconceived plan, you realize life can flow in an easier rhythm.

Once you connect with your true self, the invisible is revealed and you find meaning in your transitional experiences. Claim your wisdom and trust the promise of new beginnings.

Soulful Self-Reflection: Shining Light in the Inner Wilderness

In his insightful book *The Hidden Gospel*, Neil Douglas-Klotz writes, "If we breathe into what seems to be darkness inside, we begin to distinguish—and bring light to—different sensations and different voices inside ourselves."[63] When you gain greater knowledge of your "inner wilderness," the truths you keep hidden, it makes sense of who you truly are. Avoiding shining the light there is no better than rummaging in the darkness, since both are needed for the transformation of your consciousness.

In this meditation, I will guide you to envision the life you desire, which is aligned with your authentic self, passion and purpose.

---

63 Doulas-Klotz, *Hidden Gospel*, 77.

Find a quiet place and settle yourself. Close your eyes and place one hand lightly over your heart. Rest the other gently on your belly. Allow your breath to go deep into your diaphragm, drop your shoulders, unclench your teeth, and relax your jaw. Simply notice your breathing until the intervals between become slow and relaxed. As you breathe slowly and deeply, bring your conscious awareness into your inner wilderness.

Imagine it is dawn and you are sitting in nature, quietly observing the darkness changing into light as dawn breaks. As the sky brightens, picture yourself and your immediate surroundings moving forward to meet the sun. Allow sensation to enter your being by breathing gently and inhaling its warmth and light into your soul. Let it awaken your inner clarity and purpose.

Follow the light of your conscious awareness to where you will find opportunities and enter the realm of knowledge, intuition and transformational wisdom. Recognize patterns that no longer serve you and look for more meaningful behaviors, insights and dreams.

Shine a light on your aspirations and heart's desires. Create your vision for the future and for your life's purpose. Leave space for your inner voice to speak truths, giving clarity to your life. As you move forward, remain aware of your inner stirrings and the certainty that you are on the right path.

Reflect on these prompts:

- Did I receive clarity from my inner voice, and does it beckon me in a particular direction?
- Did I receive a new vision for my life that is worthy of my passion and purpose? If you did receive a new vision, ask yourself:
  - Does it have integrity?
  - Does it feel intuitively "right?"
  - Does it align with my authentic self and purpose?
  - Does it give me a sense of pure gratitude for being alive?

Your imagination is where you begin to envision the promise of a new beginning. When you picture what the future might look like, you formulate a plan for your new vision to become a reality.

What you wish for or create in your mind's eye will probably not manifest exactly the way you see it. You can't predict the future, after all. But you can visualize a plan for creating the life you desire and hope for.

Spend some time asking yourself these questions:

- What does my new vision look like?
- How do I see myself making it a reality?
- What choices or decisions do I need to make that will move me toward it?
- Who do I trust to be honest, supportive, encouraging and helpful that I could engage in a courageous conversation about it?
- Am I being guided to make a plan that will move me toward living my passion and purpose?

As you reflect on these questions, write down any thoughts or stirrings that emerge from your inner wilderness. Allow them to lead you deeper into the light of your soul. Trust your wisdom. When you listen to your inner stirrings, you may be surprised by the love and peace that arise from the sacred space within.

The Honoring of Sacred New Beginnings

TODAY CAN BE A TIME of honoring the sacredness of new beginnings. When transformation is required, you always have decisions to make. You can choose to remain stuck in the past or accept that, even in the midst of a catastrophe, change is a natural and necessary part of life. Your responses to its ever-shifting landscape are intimately linked to your willingness to grow and take responsibility for your actions. Resistance can lead to stagnation and fear. Refusing to acknowledge that change is inevitable will cause you great suffering. Such reluctance will prevent you from moving forward into a brighter tomorrow.

When you embrace your courage, you discover a deep peace that abides even when times are difficult and chaotic. When life tests you, empathy for yourself and others can deepen, and peace and joy can fill your heart. Once you awaken your courage and compassion, you begin to live in a generous and loving way. You engage in fewer inner dialogues where you judge or blame yourself or other people. Stripping away the layers of lies and pretenses to get down to the wild flow of energy in your soul reveals the meaning and purpose of your life. Accepting the immensity of your soul and tapping into your true nature opens the door to the inner wisdom that serves to guide you on your transformational journey. When you learn to accept mystery and uncertainty with greater ease, you courageously step into the unknown to create a new and exciting vision for your life.

Successfully navigating transitions makes you more likely to heal the emotional and psychological injuries you've suffered in the past. It can be tempting to repeat familiar patterns of behavior and old ways of relating to people, even when these actions have not served you well. When you learn to navigate tenuous transitions, you adapt and adjust to the changing territory with greater ease. Although you might not welcome the change, successfully traversing it offers many gifts, including wisdom, clarity, confidence and self-awareness. These traits empower you to invite insight and intuition as guides on your path toward wholeness.

Your years on planet Earth are not simply marked by clock time or *chronos*, but *kairos*, the ancient Greek word meaning the "right, critical or opportune moment." Life offers limitless opportunities for profound transformation, or kairos moments, whenever unexpected events occur, forcing you to look at circumstances differently. When you live with a kairos mindset, it changes how you see the world. All transitions can be exciting if you believe they bring new opportunities for creating the life you desire. They can be the right time, the critical moment, the kairos opportunity to claim a brighter tomorrow.

Transitions bring you to the edge of new beginnings that are fertile ground for fresh opportunities and dreams. As you explore the possibilities, your fears will seem to fade, and you can discard outlived, unhealthy beliefs. Over time, you gain the confidence that strengthens your courage and fortifies your stamina. Walking through the pain of change is what fosters hope for the future and faith that life can be different.

You have an inner compass that orients toward your true nature, which lives deep in the wilderness of your soul. When you become attuned to your truth, you are no longer estranged from your true nature and are completely in rhythm with yourself, everyone and everything. Once you taste this unity of consciousness, nothing else will satisfy.

But the great enigma in your quest for wholeness is that you do not have to search for home. You were there before you even started looking for it. Home is where your truest thoughts, emotions, intuitions and desires find freedom of expression. It is where you can confront your deepest questions, knowing your truth will be revealed. You may never silence all your worries or remove all the pain, but you can find peace and joy right here, right now, in this very moment.

Let your heart be open to new opportunities and adventures, and sing with joy for new beginnings. Let your spirit be open to see beyond what your mind can imagine. Live trusting that whatever presents itself will be exactly what you need. You have overcome other challenges that have provided wisdom and courage to create a new beginning. When you claim your confidence and courage, you discover a new vision for the future you long for and deserve.

Trusting the promise of new beginnings is a commitment to hope and wholeness. It is also a commitment to creativity, to curiosity, to imagination, and to gratitude for what Joseph Campbell referred to as the "rapture of being alive"—all qualities of your truest self. There is no self-compassion without passion, no self-forgiveness without suffering. No beginnings without endings. No rebirth without surrendering. When you accept transitions and the wisdom they offer, your actions align with your values and beliefs, and you reach a deep sense of peace and unity with life itself.

Chapter 12
Navigating Monumental Transitions

Throughout your lifetime, you will experience monumental transitions that have a global impact. These are times when a seismic shift occurs and life is changed forever, not just for you, but for everyone around you too. When you think back on these events later, you remember exactly where you were when the world seemed to turn upside down. These exclamation marks on your lifeline may lead you to ask others, "Where were you when _____ happened?"

For previous generations, the bombing of Pearl Harbor was one such occasion. Depending on when you were born, it might have been when President John F. Kennedy was assassinated. Or it could be when the space shuttle *Challenger* broke apart, killing all seven astronauts onboard. For many alive today, it was the 9/11 terrorist attacks. On a more global scale, the COVID-19 pandemic blindsided the world with a devastating health crisis that affected everyone on the planet.

During the pandemic, millions of people suffered and struggled to survive, engulfed by isolation and loneliness, fear and anxiety, sadness and grief. They battled against an unseen but very real enemy. The virus didn't discriminate. Its sole function was to find a host and replicate. We could no longer deny the interconnectedness of humankind—we all breathe the same air. We couldn't escape the reality that the world as we knew it was changing, and we had no road map for navigating the uncharted waters.

As the casualties mounted, we struggled to adapt to the mandates and restrictions required to stay alive and functional in a world turned upside down. Our usual avoidance tactics of reading a good book, working on an unfinished project, or binge-watching a Netflix series provided temporary escape, but there was always the ever-looming question of how to transform chaos and confusion into clarity when life changes dramatically and global transformation is called for.

We longed for our "old normal" and would have given anything to be able to do all the things we had taken for granted before and had thought would always be possible. In an age of government-enforced shutdowns, sheltering at home, social distancing, and wearing masks, just navigating daily life felt constricting. Our greatest desires were just to be able to go to work, attend school, meet a friend for coffee, join an in-person meeting, or visit a hospitalized family member or friend. The reality we were struggling to comprehend was that to stay alive, we had to remain apart. Love and fear, solidarity and distance had never been more connected.

As the months dragged on, we felt overwhelming grief, not just from the mounting deaths and illnesses, but from the loss of social contact and interactions, the loss of freedom to move about in the world, and the loss of special events. Our tears fell like rain as we grieved the collective disruptions, disturbances, disorientations and distresses brought on by the pandemic.

Consumed by the constant grief, fear and anxiety, we gave in to anger and frustration. This eventually led to refusals and protests against government mandates, creating increased anger and divisiveness among family and friends—adding to an already tense environment.

Despite all the chaos and confusion, all the disorder and disruption, all the grief and anger, people came together in ways we could not have imagined years earlier. Around the world, citizens discovered creative and caring ways to support one another while remaining safe. The nightly news bore witness as people gathered at the end of hospital shifts to celebrate frontline workers as they returned home after another long, exhausting day caring for patients. Relatives gathered outside hospital and nursing home windows to wave to quarantined loved ones. Neighbors serenaded each other from their balconies, showing solidarity by raising their voices in song together.

Family and friends, unable to gather for birthdays, graduations and holidays, celebrated in driveways and with drive-by parades, where they sang, honked horns, and waved festive signs from inside vehicles. We witnessed the strength of the human spirit as the world came together in creative and compassionate ways to encourage one another amid this overwhelmingly disorienting and disruptive time of global crisis.

When fear and uncertainty peaked, the world demonstrated a heightened sense of compassion. Neighbors extended simple acts of kindness and selflessness to their fellow human beings. While families sheltered at home, they reported spending time together, playing board games, cooking meals, learning new hobbies or life skills, sharing stories, or simply cooperating with household responsibilities. Friends delivered meals, wrote cheerful personal notes, and greeted elderly or ill neighbors with birthday wishes and holiday carols. The pandemic taught us that kindness and compassion are powers we all have—we just needed to use them.

When monumental transitions occur, whether on a global or more regional scale, we are forced to confront our human condition. In the midst of widespread suffering, people extend empathy and compassion to one another and gain a deep understanding of the need for solidarity with their fellow human beings. Unity allows us to gain courage and hope, knowing we are not alone. We are all interconnected. And when we realize we are in this together, we can make it through turbulent times.

Solidarity and Shared Compassion

FEELING INTERCONNECTED CALLS US OUT of isolation into community. Only when we are in solidarity with all of creation can humankind survive. Compassion requires depth of soul and a capacity for empathy. These two qualities, compassion and solidarity, are what bind us together into an ocean of love.

During catastrophic events and man-made tragedies, people have demonstrated how a city, state or nation can unite in the face of horrific circumstances. Together, we find refuge and strength in solidarity and shared compassion.

I know this happened during the Oklahoma City bombing, which took place in my home state on April 19, 1995, when a truck bomb was used to destroy the Alfred P. Murrah Federal Building in downtown Oklahoma City. It was the first large-scale domestic terrorist attack on American soil, killing 168 innocent souls, 19 of whom were children, and injuring hundreds more. At the time of this writing, it remains the deadliest act of domestic terrorism in US history.

If you and I were to sit and have a cup of coffee one day and share where we were at the time of this event, the story you might have to tell of that day will vary from mine. This is mostly because we're different individuals with different perspectives. But it's also partly because of my proximity to the event. When you're more distant from the epicenter of a catastrophe, a secondhand recounting of it will always differ from a firsthand experience.

I vividly remember where I was that fateful Wednesday morning at 9:02 a.m. At home, north of Stillwater, approximately 80 miles from Oklahoma City, I was preparing to go to work when I heard a thundering boom and felt the windows pulse. I went outside to see if an airplane had caused the sound, but the sky was empty. When I turned on the television, I learned there had been an explosion at the Murrah Building. I immediately called the office of the Oklahoma Psychological Association to have my name put on the list of volunteers.

During the next several weeks, I served at the family center located in the First Christian Church on North Walker in Oklahoma City. I assisted a representative from the medical examiner's office with five death notifications for families of the victims, conducted several debriefings with the death notification volunteers, and provided mental health triage and support services to survivors of the bombing and families of victims.

On May 5, 1995, recovery efforts at the bomb site were discontinued due to the instability of the Murrah Building and the safety risk to recovery teams. On that date, I assisted in the death notification of Christy Rosas, age twenty-two, whose body could not be recovered. The mother of a five-year-old son had only been employed at the Federal Employees Credit Union for three weeks. Her husband, parents, grandparents, pastor and several other family members were present for the death notification. They expressed to me their concerns about how and what to tell her son regarding the death of his mother, how to assist him with his grief, and what signs and symptoms they should be aware of regarding his emotional health and well-being.

The FBI gave the family special clearance to visit Ground Zero for a private memorial service. The police chaplain accompanied them to the spot where they believed Christy's body was located. Her family spontaneously constructed a monument of rubble, where they placed yellow roses, her favorite flower, and the chaplain offered a loving tribute in her memory.

Almost a month later, on May 23, workers brought down the Alfred P. Murrah Federal Building with an explosion of nearly one hundred pounds of dynamite. Six days after that, workers recovered the bodies of three more bombing victims from the rubble.[64] Christy Rosas was among them.

Like many who witnessed the tragic destruction and emotional devastation of this senseless act, the Oklahoma City bombing affected me deeply, both personally and professionally. Consequently, my clinical practice became focused primarily on treating post-traumatic stress disorder.

During this tragedy, Oklahomans demonstrated that even in the midst of suffering and chaos, solidarity sustains, strengthens and provides space for shared compassion to unite people. The values that soon were formulated into the Oklahoma Standard were on full display after the bombing. This statewide initiative preserves and promotes a culture of caring citizens by encouraging acts of service, honor and kindness. Even before the initiative was codified, Oklahomans were pulling together to get through this challenging time.

Weeks before the last bodies were recovered, a prayer service was held in Oklahoma City on Sunday, April 23, 1995. Dr. Billy Graham spoke and offered the following words:

> Times like this will do one of two things. They will either make us hard and bitter and angry at God, or they will make us tender and open, and help us reach out in trust and faith. ... A tragedy like this could have torn this city apart, but instead it has united you in a way that you've never been united before. ... The forces of hate and violence must not be allowed to gain their victory—not just in our society, but in our hearts.

---

64 *Requiem for the Heartland: The Oklahoma City Bombing*. (The Tides Foundation and Collins Publishers, 1995), 119.

Nor must we respond to hate with more hate. This is a time of coming together and we've seen that already and have been inspired by it.[65]

The unity we shared continues to this day. In 2025, during the thirtieth anniversary observance of the Oklahoma City bombing, the state and our nation remembered how, in a moment of horrific devastation and senseless tragedy, citizens of all races, political affiliations, and religious beliefs came together to respond with shared compassion. In solidarity, citizens were able to put aside their disagreements, dogmatic opinions, and judgmental differences. Oklahomans were strong for one another, so no one felt alone.

The theme for the remembrance ceremony was "A Day of Darkness. Years of Light." The service was held at First Church, which had served as the makeshift morgue where families came to identify their loved ones' remains. Former President Bill Clinton, in office at the time of the bombing, was the keynote speaker. He recalled how Oklahoma City came together and responded with empathy and unity, and noted that the Oklahoma Standard remains alive today and is needed in the world now more than ever.

Shared compassion requires the inner strength to be with another person and be present with their feelings without losing yourself. It involves holding their painful thoughts and feelings in mindful awareness rather than over-identifying with them. A kindhearted person is able to respond to difficult and chaotic events with empathy. Compassion born out of your own suffering makes you more aware of that of others.

Cultivating shared compassion starts with extending love and kindness to yourself, then adds the strong desire to ease the suffering of other human beings, inviting you to enter their world. You must recognize the other person's pain in your own heart. An empathetic person says, "I am fragile and mortal, just like you. I, too, have felt pain. I, too, have been afraid. I, too, have been wounded and suffered loss." Shared compassion asks you to go where it hurts, to enter the pain, to share the brokenness, fear and anguish. To bear witness in the hour of grief by being present, even when nothing can be done to change the outcome. To share the loneliness, fear, confusion and woundedness, you

---

65 "Billy Graham: A Voice of Hope in Crisis—Oklahoma City, 1995," *The Billy Graham Library*, accessed July 1, 2025, emeraldlakebooks.com/ntgraham.

must be vulnerable with the vulnerable and powerless with the powerless. You can be compassionate *only* when you are honestly willing to recognize and confess your own humanity.

Solidarity and shared compassion are intimate avenues for healing life's greatest suffering, not by removing or forgetting it, but by extending empathy with your fellow human beings. Despite the discomfort, do not forget your history or deny your tragedies. It is important to remember, acknowledge and learn from the past. Compassion is the ground from which solidarity grows. It is through deep empathy and unity of purpose that you gain the courage to hold your own struggles and sorrows in your heart while connecting with the suffering and heartache of others. During shared tragedies, solidarity and compassion are made visible, opening you up to hope, which depends on your willingness to go where grief, anger, fear, shame and woundedness exist.

The pandemic provided an opportunity to ask ourselves these two deeply meaningful and critical questions:

- What kind of world do we want for ourselves and for future generations?
- Do we want to move toward a world that is kinder, gentler and more compassionate?

When we strive to come together with love and kindness, we become part of the hope and healing that can transform adversity into connection. Change begins within, when one person chooses to be compassionate, igniting the flames for a new vision that unites all humanity. It may be time to search inward for shared compassion and love, to heal old wounds, and to acknowledge and trust the universal truths that bind us together.

Hope for a Brighter Tomorrow

HOPE CAN PROVIDE STABILITY for your soul every time the events of your life or the suffering in the world bring chaos and anxiety, sadness and grief, isolation and loneliness. It is not optimism. Hopeful people see the hard reality of human existence but are not imprisoned by it. They suffer like everyone else, yet they do not hold on to pain. There will always be difficulties where doubt and fear emerge. But living with optimism allows you to trust that positive things beyond your imagination will happen and to live creatively in the present.

Living a hopeful life, you carry the message of unity and compassion to others. This doesn't mean pretending that suffering doesn't exist, but bringing a helping hand to the downtrodden and a smile to the lonely—letting them know they are not alone. Hope is what keeps faith and love alive when it is so desperately needed.

Hope is life-giving. It doesn't allow you to become a victim of despair. Instead, it empowers you to be strong in the face of adversity.

In a world filled with so much divisiveness and chaos, created by both external and internal forces, we are at a critical moment when change is needed. Just as personal transformation begins within your own heart and mind, so does the work of global transformation. While it may be triggered by a monumental event or something that hits closer to home, each of us is responsible to contribute to this shift. You must be the change you seek. The question is: "How can we find opportunities for meaningful change that unites humanity during uninvited global events?"

Civil Rights icon and Congressman John Lewis spoke about a vision of a "beloved community" where everyone can achieve justice and fulfill their potential as human beings.[66] Building such a community is about cultivating love, which can heal and create unity when we seek to empty ourselves of our differences. When we are devoid of anger and fear, it allows us to grasp the joy and peace that can bond us.

Practicing solidarity and shared compassion can radically alter our vision for life because we become more concerned about unity rather than petty things that, in the end, don't really matter. When we treat our neighbor as ourselves, we are fulfilling our calling as members of a shared beloved community. Searching for meaning and truth requires significant strength, courage and empathy from all of us. As Mother Teresa reminded us, "Not all of us can do great things. But we can do small things with great love."

Similar to other times in history when there has been tremendous tension, the world seems to be at a tipping point. Whether the changes will be for the better is yet unknown. It will take all of us—every nation, every race, every

---

66 John Lewis, *Across That Bridge: A Vision for Change and the Future of America* (Hachette Books, 2012), 12.

religion—to effect positive outcomes. Until we truly recognize and embody the interdependence of all humanity, none of us will experience hope and healing. We must come together for the greater good of all people and the earth. We must be voices of wisdom to promote loving-kindness and shared compassion. Now is the time for transformation.

Today, ask yourself:

- What would the world look like if it was transformed by the renewal of our minds so we all lived in harmony with one another?
- How can people, despite their differences, come together, care about one another, be compassionate toward each other, and become united in one purpose for the greater good of all?
- What is my role as a responsible citizen in transforming our planet into a more just, luminous, compassionate and united world?

During times of overwhelming tumult, you must look deep within your soul for wisdom. You cannot change what is going on in the outer world, but you can adjust what goes on within yourself. When you shine the light of hope into the darkness, you can be transformed for the better. Each of us has an opportunity to choose to act with loving-kindness and compassion or to continue in a state of chaos and confusion, anger and division.

It is our responsibility as spiritual beings to be involved in making our world a better place. Allowing our lives to be used to transform anger into love, division into unity, and to manifest compassion is a goal worthy of pursuit. When we open our hearts and minds to receive spiritual truths, our love will be genuine and can be used to transform the world with mutual respect and dignity.

We have the capacity to heal the suffering world when we welcome all of humanity with singleness of purpose and loving-kindness. The struggles will only be worth the effort when we are all willing to commit to whatever it takes to build a more compassionate and united world.

Chapter 13
Moving Forward with Wisdom

As you've read this book, you've traveled inward through seasons of loss, renewal and growth. You've explored the nature of transition, the wisdom of the soul, and the courage it takes to face change with an open heart. Along the way, you've been invited to listen more deeply, to let go of outdated roles and beliefs, and to awaken your inner knowing.

Through soulful reflection, I hope you have uncovered hidden truths, gained new insights, and gently reclaimed parts of yourself that had long been silenced or forgotten. The path may not have been easy, but the commitment to walk it with intention, compassion and spiritual curiosity has already begun to shape you from within.

Perhaps you now see more clearly how your inner and outer transitions are woven together and how wisdom can emerge from even the most difficult moments. You've learned to honor your natural rhythms, listen to your breath, and find stillness amid uncertainty. You've also discovered that transformation does not require having all the answers—it simply asks you to show up, again and again, with courage and curiosity.

Transitions always involve the falling away of what once was, creating space for something new to emerge even as something familiar ends. But beginnings don't often arrive with fanfare. They unfold slowly, sometimes invisibly, deep beneath the surface. Trust that the fruit of your inner work is taking root.

Let your breath guide you. Let your soul lead you. Let each small act of alignment become a seed planted in sacred ground. Whether you are moving through grief, uncertainty, renewal or joy, the wisdom you've gained as you've learned to navigate these transitions will continue to speak—quietly, persistently and always in service of your becoming your authentic self.

The Art of Beginnings

NONE OF US HAS A PREORDAINED SCRIPT for how the world will be; nor do we know what lies ahead or why certain things happen. Life moves forward even in the face of the unknown. There can be no growth if you don't remain open and vulnerable to not having all the answers right now. An integral part of inner transformation is learning to trust the process.

Sometimes, beginning the journey is the toughest part. If you want something new to happen, you must be willing to let go of your expectations of how you wish life could be and risk stepping into the unknown. Consider this: Would you have begun this exploration if you had known when you started reading this book how deep you would be digging within your soul to gain the wisdom you now possess?

The thrill of self-discovery, the integration of insight, and the peace of inner knowing can happen only when you risk taking that first step. To live creatively, you must discern where life has become stagnant and where something new may be ripening. Promise and excitement emerge when you risk venturing ahead. The wisdom of an old Irish proverb advises, "A good beginning is half the work." Sometimes the greatest challenge is just to begin.

Transitions aways involve the falling away of things as they have been, and welcoming new things yet to be revealed. With any birthing process, gestation is necessary for the right timing of something to be revealed. Like birth pains, what seems like an obstacle becomes a door; what appears to be a hindrance becomes a way forward. In this moment of clarity, beginnings become opportunities for the excitement that comes with new life.

Wisdom will come when the time is right. When the soul is ready for a fresh start, your inner knowing will recognize the right direction and invite you to begin. When you have hope for what is to come, you can experience joy amid the uncertainty of what lies ahead. Choosing hope is choosing joy.

Considerable time may be required before a new path opens to welcome you. In the meantime, find the courage to remain true to your inner voice. Ask yourself:

- What is the new horizon that desires recognition now?
- Am I ready to move forward with the next step on my transformational journey?

I encourage you to continue your quest for wholeness; to be who you were born to be and to live a purposeful life. Share this wisdom with others. Infuse every day with passion and meaning. What joy that will bring to you and the world!

It has been an honor to accompany you on this exploration of self-discovery. I hope the rewards and insights the expedition has brought you have been worth the effort. May the information and practices outlined in *Navigating Transitions* open a pathway for you to embrace change and allow you to build a foundation for conquering all the transitions you will encounter throughout your lifetime.

It is my humble wish that you discover the joy that comes from claiming the life-affirming truths about your authentic self, and that your courage and compassion enable you to create a life that is aligned with your unique purpose.

Thank you for reading *Navigating Transitions*.
If you've enjoyed reading this book, please leave a review on your favorite review site. In doing so, you can help reach more readers who might benefit from it.

Discussion Guide

These questions are designed to help you pause and reflect on what you've read, so you can learn what you can from the transitions you've already been through. They may be used for personal journaling, in a support or study group, or in conversation with a trusted friend, mentor or therapist.

There is no right or wrong way to approach them. Some questions may speak to you immediately, while others may feel more difficult or call for more time. You might choose to respond in writing, sit quietly with them in contemplation, or talk them through in community with others.

The goal is not to answer every question but to listen for what resonates with your own experience. Trust that your inner wisdom will guide you toward the reflections most needed for this season of your journey.

Chapter 1. Understanding Life's Transformations

1. *Navigating Transitions* describes change as a natural and inevitable part of life that offers wisdom and hope for claiming your purpose and living authentically.
    - What have been some of your most difficult transitions?
    - How have you changed?
    - What wisdom did you gain?
    - If you are in the midst of a life crisis, can you view it as an opportunity for transforming adversity into inner truth?

2. The concept of your "seed of selfhood" relates to the spiritual DNA of your true self and unique purpose. In the self-reflective exercise, Claiming Your Birthright Nature on page 11:
   - Did you connect with or claim unique characteristics of your authentic self?
   - How can this insight help guide your journey toward wholeness?

Chapter 2. Beginnings and Endings

3. We will all experience "necessary losses" when life changes and we must face the pain of change.
   - How do you respond when something ends and you must look at life differently?
   - Do you deny or resist the inevitable? Or do you gather your courage to forge a new path?
   - Do you ask yourself: *Who am I now at this new phase in my life?* and *How can I chart a new vision for my future?*
4. During childhood, were your feelings labeled as good or bad, right or wrong, acceptable or unacceptable?
   - If so, how do these messages affect you today?
   - Are you able to accept the full spectrum of your emotions without judgement?
   - What would allow you to express your feelings honestly and listen to the wisdom of your own heart?

Chapter 3. Reclaiming Your Authentic Self

5. Our beliefs about relationships are typically formulated during childhood. Patterns such as perfectionism, people-pleasing or assuming responsibility for others may once have helped you but now hold you back.
   - Where did these beliefs come from?
   - Who do they serve today?
   - What are your own beliefs?
   - What actions can you take to adjust or release any unhealthy internalized beliefs or self-sabotaging relationship patterns?

6. Healthy boundaries are essential for authentic relationships.
    - Can you maintain effective boundaries when necessary?
    - If not, what makes setting appropriate limits difficult for you?
    - How could your relationships be different if you could maintain healthy boundaries?
    - In the Setting Clear Boundaries Exercise on page 33, we explore dynamics to consider. What changes could you implement to strengthen your relationships?

Chapter 4. Hearing Your Inner Voice

7. How do you connect with your inner voice?
    - Are you able to tune out your inner critic and listen to your truth?
    - What does this Sufi adage mean to you: "Each person has a unique note in the universal symphony, no one else can strike yours except you"?
    - How can you claim your one precious voice and hear your true song?
8. Chapter 4 emphasizes being present, listening attentively, and speaking intentionally.
    - Do you have trouble sitting quietly, without speaking, and truly listening to another person?
    - Do you feel safe speaking your inner truth with intention? If not, how could practicing courageous conversations help you build the skills necessary for healthy and meaningful dialogue?

Chapter 5. Trusting the Unfolding

9. Transitions ask us to surrender the past, release old patterns of relating, readjust priorities, and search for new opportunities to nourish our mind, body and spirit.
    - What needs pruning during this season in your life?
    - How can you create space to explore a new vision of the future?
    - What would it look like to flourish to your full potential?

Chapter 6. Bridging Endings to New Beginnings

10. How connected are you with your intuitive self?
    - Do you trust your intuition and recognize synchronicities?

- Do you pay attention to your dreams?
- What would it be like to adopt an attitude of curiosity and introspection?
- How could your intuitive self guide you during times of change?

11. Silence and solitude can help reconnect you to your inner being.
    - What would it be like to have a day of silence and solitude?
    - Do you have any fears or concerns about solitude?
    - Does your environment provide a space for soothing your soul?
    - Can you create your own sacred refuge for restoring yourself physically, emotionally and spiritually?
    - How might such a space help you connect with your true self?

Chapter 7. Nurturing Harmony in the Everyday

12. Everyday life offers many chances for harmony and balance.
    - What daily practices help you stay grounded?
    - Where do you notice tension in your external environment?
    - How could you invite more peace and harmony into space around you?
    - How might the two simple breath exercises help you manage your everyday stressors and improve your mind/body connection?

Chapter 8. Practicing Inner Knowing Through Contemplation

13. Meditation, contemplation, reading poetry, and journaling are practices designed to strengthen your connection with your inner knowing.
    - Which practices appeal to you most?
    - How could you make them part of your daily routine?
    - How could the meditative and contemplative practices increase your awareness of your spiritual self?
    - How might poetry help you explore your authentic self, soothe your soul, and connect with your inner knowing?
    - How could developing a journaling practice help you gain insight and wisdom for healing emotional wounds and embracing new beginnings?

Chapter 9. Accepting Change, Trusting the Soul

14. Life's challenges are often interconnected.
    - What coping skills and insights have you learned that help you adapt when change occurs?
    - What "threads of continuity" provide comfort and assurance to your soul during turbulent times?
15. Your future is shaped in part by the choices you make.
    - How does aligning your moral compass with your true self guide your decisions?
    - What is one choice you can make now that would move you closer to the life you desire and deserve?

Chapter 10. Transforming Through Adversity

16. Adversity can be our greatest teacher in our quest for wholeness.
    - How do you view the idea that everything that happens is part of your life journey?
    - Have you experienced a devastating loss that has provided transitional wisdom?
    - If so, what insights did you gain that gave your life new purpose and meaning?
17. The art of inner alchemy transforms outdated aspects of yourself into wisdom and strength by relinquishing them to the fire to be turned into gold.
    - What treasures did you uncover while "digging in the ashes"?
    - How have these gifts helped you to gain the wisdom of your authentic self?
    - Did claiming who you truly are bring you "the rapture of being alive"?
    - How will this be helpful as you envision this next phase of your journey?

Chapter 11. Exploring Passion, Purpose and New Territory

18. Even life's darkest storms carry the promise of new beginnings.
    - How does knowing what excites you and brings you alive provide clues to your purpose?
    - How does joy point you toward what matters most?

- What is one thing you can commit to pursuing that will move you closer to living with joy and passion?

Chapter 12. Navigating Monumental Transitions

19. Solidarity and shared compassion are intimate avenues for healing monumental transitions, and they can radically alter our vision for the kind of world we want for ourselves and for future generations.
    - How can you extend empathy and promote loving-kindness to your fellow human beings?
    - What would the world be like if we lived in harmony despite our differences?
    - What role can you play in helping create a more just, compassionate and united world?

Acknowledgments

I am deeply grateful to Tara R. Alemany for her splendid editing, publishing expertise, generous guidance, and patient dedication in transforming my manuscript into the book you are holding. She provided clarity, an orderly structure, and constant support that have benefited the development of this book. It is a joy to work with her and Emerald Lake Books.

This book began as conversations with my dear friend, Carol Bender, who introduced me to yoga and the chakras. These talks sparked our collaboration to weave together Western psychology and Eastern philosophy to create a series of seven workshops for awakening and balancing the body, mind and spirit. How we birthed a new workshop every month is still a mystery! *Navigating Transitions* exists because of our early collaboration. Thank you for your continuous support and trusted counsel. The bond we share is a blessing.

My deepest gratitude goes to my three brave friends who so generously shared their personal transition stories to enrich and enlighten the book. Their courage, openness and resilience shine through in their words.

My heartfelt gratitude to Sara Schnekloth, who entered my life at a time when I was eager to explore the creative side of my brain. Her gifted teaching style inspires making beautiful art and embracing joyful living. I am thankful for her early reading of the introduction. Her inspiring comments reinforced my hope and desire to write a book that could benefit those seeking their true nature.

I am thankful too to Lee Bird and Judi Baker for their early review of the manuscript, their helpful feedback, and their continuous encouragement throughout this long process. Now it's time to celebrate!

I owe a great deal of gratitude to all my clients, colleagues, instructors and mentors who have taught me deep insights through their dedication to personal growth and their courage to search inward for sacred truths that give life purpose and meaning. Gratitude goes also to my spiritual guides, many of whom are quoted in the text, who have brought depth and wisdom to my writing and to my life.

And finally, I want to express my love and heartfelt thanks to all my family and friends whose lives have enriched and blessed me through all the changing seasons. Special thanks to my longtime Aspen friends, who have been my guiding light and constant source of strength through the many transitions we have shared. Deep gratitude to my book club for cheering me on when the writing became tedious and my stamina wavered, and especially for your generous offer to host a book launch event. Each of your trusted relationships has provided clarity regarding what matters most in my quest for living life wholeheartedly.

About the Author

Linda Burks, PhD, is a licensed psychologist whose area of expertise and specialized training is working with post-traumatic stress disorder. She brings over four decades of experience as a psychotherapist to her first book, *Navigating Transitions*.

In her clinical practice, she observed that people typically enter therapy after some type of life-changing event or turbulent transition unravels their sense of stability, forcing them to understand their life differently. Recognizing this prompted Linda to offer hope and encouragement to all who seek to know their true nature and to live wholeheartedly with passion and purpose.

Through her company, Calibrating Your Compass, Linda offered workshops designed to ignite inner wisdom; teach healing practices to nourish and awaken the body, mind and spirit; connect with your authentic self; and create a foundation for being who you truly are and living the life you envision more purposefully.

Yet even in her retirement, Linda still prioritizes enriching and expanding people's understanding of how life's struggles can awaken consciousness and illuminate a path for those who seek meaning and purpose in life. She does this through her speaking, teaching and writing in the hope that those she meets will discover their inner strength, life-affirming truths, and courage and compassion to live life to its fullest.

Linda lives in Stillwater, Oklahoma, where she writes, enjoys painting and yoga classes, and explores new adventures on her bucket list.

If you're interested in having Linda speak to your group or organization, you can contact her at emeraldlakebooks.com/burks.

For more great books, please visit us at
emeraldlakebooks.com.

www.ingramcontent.com/pod-product-compliance
Lightning Source LLC
Chambersburg PA
CBHW061807070526
44586CB00024B/2755